THE WALK SERIES

HE LEADS ME BESIDE STILL WATERS

STEVE GALLAGHER

"Purity for Life"

www.purelifeministries.org

888.PURELIFE

Also available by Steve Gallagher:

A Lamp Unto My Feet
At the Altar of Sexual Idolatry
At the Altar of Sexual Idolatry Workbook
A Biblical Guide to Counseling the Sexual Addict
How America Lost Her Innocence
Intoxicated with Babylon
Irresistible to God
Living in Victory
Out of the Depths of Sexual Sin
Pressing On Toward the Heavenly Calling
Standing Firm Through the Great Apostasy
The Walk of Repentance

For these books and other teaching materials please contact:

Pure Life Ministries

14 School Street
Dry Ridge, KY 41035
(888) PURELIFE - to order
(859) 824-4444
(859) 813-0005 FAX
www.purelifeministries.org

EAN 978-0-9800286-0-7
ISBN 0-9800286-0-4

www.purelifeministries.org
888.PURELIFE

HE LEADS
ME BESIDE
STILL WATERS

I dedicate this book to
Greg, one of my dearest friends.
Thanks so much for always believing the best.

HE LEADS
ME BESIDE
STILL WATERS

CONTENTS

INTRODUCTION

The actual title of the book of Psalms in the original language is *sepher thillim*, "the book of praises." This is an apt name, as the adoration of God is such a prominent theme throughout the book. One old-time writer stated, "The book begins with benediction, and ends with praise - first, blessing to man, and then glory to God."[1]

Unquestionably, the Psalter contains some of the richest passages found in Scripture. C.S. Lewis spoke for countless saints when he wrote: "The most valuable thing the Psalms do for me is to express that same delight in God which made David dance... I find an experience fully God-centered, asking of God no gift more urgently than His presence, the gift of Himself, joyous to the highest degree, and unmistakably real."[2]

In a day when one can easily while away hours titillating the flesh with the worldly fare offered on television or the Internet, the importance of possessing inspired literature which can turn our thoughts heavenward cannot be overstated. No other portion of Scripture is so capable of ushering the hungry soul into the presence of God as this compilation of ancient Hebraic songs.

As has already been noted, the worship of Jehovah is one of the primary subjects covered in the book of Psalms. The authors* address God's glorious attributes in a variety of ways. His sovereignty, majesty, power, mercy, compassion and trustworthiness are all emphasized in different parts of the book. One cannot read Psalms without walking away with a more lofty perspective of the Lord. Nowhere in this book does one encounter the disrespectful and flippant attitude toward the Lord that is practiced in much of today's Church. Every word penned emits the aroma of humble worship and reverential fear.

Perhaps what stands out above all else is the sense that the reader is allowed inside the most intimate thoughts of these dear saints of old. "The whole inner life of the pious man is laid open," says one commentator.[3] It is "a record of the workings of the heart," states another.[4]

The book of Psalms brings the lives of biblical heroes down to our level—where we are provided a forthright glimpse into their minds. When David opens up about his deepest fears, one can see that he, too, "was a man with a nature like ours." (James 5:17) When Asaph expresses his indignation over the fact that the Lord allows the wicked to prosper, we find a God who is willing to allow questions to be raised about His fairness. When others upbraid the wicked or share their most private doubts, the reader is witnessing the uncontrived feelings experienced by the writer.

Through it all one cannot escape the fact that the book of Psalms is an utterly candid compilation of the mental struggles of these different men; of their varying seasons of joy, anguish and despair; of their highest hopes and deepest fears; of their conflicts or even failures with sin; of their disgust for self-serving flatterers and their compassion for the needy; and most of all, for their overarching appreciation for the Lord's sovereign involvement in their lives.

The book of Psalms is a treasure chest of the most profound interactions between pious men and a loving, caring God. David, its most prominent writer, was called a man after God's own heart. What could be more beneficial and rewarding than to contemplate his times of intimate communion with a holy God?

A study of such a book as this deserves one's utmost effort. With that in mind, I would like to offer a few suggestions that I believe will help the reader maximize the benefits of this study through the choicest Psalms:

First, prayerfully approach each day's lessons. The Lord will speak to you and implant His wisdom in your heart if you will but ask Him. You do not need more biblical knowledge; you need a divine impartation! If you will ask, seek and knock,

---

* Some authorities believe that every psalm was written by David. According to their theory, those ascribed to other writers were either compiled and used by them (e.g., Asaph, the sons of Korah, et al) or dedicated to them (e.g., Solomon). Athanasius (296-373) claimed that Hezekiah's scholars chose 150 out of 3,000 psalms penned by David. It is possible that his opinion came from having access to writings that have since been lost. Conversely, evidence indicates that a number of the psalms were written at a much later period of time (i.e., during the exile in Babylon).

unexpected doors will be opened to you through Scripture. Approach the Word with expectancy and faith!

Second, be ever mindful that you live in a world that lies under a satanic enchantment. Spiritual darkness pervades our culture. The intoxicating voice of darkness blares at you relentlessly through television, radio and the Internet. It appears as truth, but is actually laced with underlying false messages, cunningly cloaked in seemingly innocuous information. The Bible is the one existing source of pure *truth*. Humble yourself before it and treat it with the utmost reverence.

Third, spend as much time as you can in your studies. You probably don't realize how much you have been polluted by the spirit of this world.† The more time you spend soaking in Scripture, the more you will take on the mind of God. Conversely, the more you immerse yourself in the world, the more its standards and values will shape your thinking and desires.

If you feel as though you have already been terribly contaminated, don't despair! The Word of God can and will straighten out faulty perspectives, skewed attitudes and unlawful desires. You need only immerse yourself in it, allowing it to do its supernatural work inside you. David said it himself: "The law of the Lord is perfect, restoring the soul…" (Psalm 19:7)

Practical Considerations

Before you begin, there are a few things to consider about the study. Each week will cover various psalms. Make sure that you prayerfully read each day's featured psalm. You will also notice a supplemental reading: a pertinent chapter from the Bible for you to read if you want to spend more time studying after completing that day's lesson. Occasionally, you will be asked to look up a Hebrew word in a Bible dictionary. This can be a thorough reference book such as the *Theological Wordbook of the Old Testament* or the simpler *Strong's Hebrew Dictionary* found on many computer Bible programs.

In some studies, I offer different Bible translations or paraphrases which provide a fresh perspective on key verses for that week's study. Since our book of Psalms is translated from a different language, no single translation will always capture the full sense of what was being expressed. Sometimes the student will gain a much richer comprehension of a verse by reading it in a variety of translations. A list of the different versions utilized may be found in the Appendix at the back of this book.

The purpose of Sunday's homework is to challenge the reader to personally apply what he or she has learned from the week's lessons (which explains why they may, at times, seem disjointed).

Finally, I want to encourage you to put your heart into each day's lesson. For instance, when you are asked to look up various passages and tell what you learn from them, try to resist the temptation to impatiently rewrite what has been stated. Think about what is being expressed in that verse, carefully pondering each word. Consider the verse in light of the psalm you are studying. Most of all, prayerfully ask the Lord to open the Word to your heart.

The months that I have spent meditating upon this incredible book have been greatly enriching and tremendously inspiring. I hope that by the end of the next twelve weeks, you too will be able to say with conviction, *He Leads Me Beside Still Waters*!

---

† For an exhaustive study on how the spirit of this world is affecting believers, please see my book, *Intoxicated with Babylon*.

WEEK I: THE RIGHTEOUS AND THE GODLESS

Monday

1. Read and meditate on Psalm 1 (supplemental reading: I John 2).

2. One would expect the book of Psalms to open with a rich description of life in God, but surprisingly, it opens with a negative statement. It doesn't say what the blessed man does but what he doesn't do. It is simply a fact that the Christian life is as much about what you don't do as it is about what you do. No matter what positive things you may do to seek God, your efforts will be nullified if you keep the door open for the enemy. Write out Psalm 1:1.

3. The psalmist indicates three definite progressions in Psalm 1:1. They are indicated by verbs and nouns. The verbs indicate the type of activity involved (walk, stand, sit). The nouns describe what the activity is involved in (counsel, path, seat) and the type of people involved (ungodly, sinners, scoffers).

   In reading the poetical books of the Old Testament, it is important to understand that the Jewish writers had a different style of writing than we employ. For instance, it is very common to find verses in Psalms and Proverbs that contain two phrases making the exact same point using different terms or, at other times, the two phrases will describe opposite subjects (e.g., righteous, godless).

   In Psalm 1:1, the author uses a less common "Hebraism." It is the linking of verbs and nouns together in a way that should not be taken beyond their original intention. In other words, in the Jewish mind, these different terms were interchangeable with each other.

   Choose one of the nouns employed in Psalm 1:1 and write out the verse using only that noun in each of the phrases (e.g., "*How blessed is the man who does not walk in the counsel of the <u>wicked</u>, nor stand in the path of the <u>wicked</u>, nor sit in the seat of the <u>wicked</u>.*")

4. Notice the progression of nouns in Psalm 1:1. I will provide a working definition of these nouns. Please describe in your own words how these definitions help you to understand what the psalmist was saying.

   Counsel - Mindset; maxims, ruling principles; perspectives one can expect from such people.

Monday - continued

Path - Lifestyle; patterns of behavior; the general course of a person's life.

Seat - The Hebrew word (*mowshab*$_{4186}$) is usually employed to describe the place where one dwells. This is what he has settled into in life.

5. Rewrite Psalm 1:1 utilizing some of the synonyms or definitions found in the preceding question.

6. Read the following commentary by Albert Barnes and describe what you learn.

    There is, first, casual walking with the wicked, or accidentally falling into their company; there is then a more deliberate inclination for their society, indicated by a voluntary putting of oneself in places where they usually congregate, and standing to wait for them; and then there is a deliberate and settled purpose of associating with them, or of becoming permanently one of them, by regularly sitting among them.[1]

Tuesday

1. Read and meditate on Psalm 1 (supplemental reading: Ephesians 2).

2. Yesterday we looked at the type of activity mentioned in Psalm 1:1. Today we will examine the three types of people he mentioned. The first we will look at are "the wicked," (NASB, NIV) or "ungodly" (KJV, NKJV). Please describe in your own words what you learn from the following definition.

   The Wicked - This is a description of those who live without God. They aren't necessarily people involved in evil behavior; they simply live their lives without any sense of concern about God or eternal issues.

3. Look up the following verses and explain what you learn about the ungodly.

   Psalm 32:10

   Psalm 36:1

   Proverbs 3:33

   Proverbs 5:22

   Proverbs 15:9

4. Please describe in your own words what you learn from the following definition.

   Sinners - People who are actively engaging in some form of behavior clearly prohibited by Scripture.

Tuesday - continued

5. Matthew Henry wrote: "When the services of religion are laid aside, they come to be *sinners*, that is, they break out into open rebellion against God and engage in the service of sin and Satan."[2] How does his interpretation of "sinners" line up with what you typically hear in the Church today? Explain your answer.

6. Please describe in your own words what you learn from the following definition.

Scoffers - Mockers; those who hold a flippant attitude about the things of God and minimize the dangers and wrongfulness of sin. Over time they become hardened in their rebellion to God's authority until eventually they come to hold Him in contempt.

7. The book of Proverbs has much to say about scoffers. Using the following summations, write out your own description of this person.

- Delight in their scoffing (Proverbs 1:22)
- Dishonors and hates the wise man who attempts to reprove him (Proverbs 9:7-8)
- Will have to bear the weight of his behavior (Proverbs 9:12)
- Cannot find wisdom (Proverbs 14:6)
- Mocks at sin (Proverbs 14:9)
- Will face judgment (Proverbs 19:29)
- Is full of pride (Proverbs 21:24)
- Causes strife (Proverbs 22:10)
- Is an abomination to mankind (Proverbs 24:9)

Wednesday

1. Read and meditate on Psalm 1 (supplemental reading: Ecclesiastes 2).

2. Write out Psalm 1:2-3.

3. The following is my paraphrase of Psalm 1:1-3. Read this passage and write out what fresh insights or perspectives you gain.

   "Oh, the spiritual blessing that comes to the man who avoids the soul-deadening influences of the world: the realm of rebels who are flippant about the things of God and are given over to sin. One of the great pleasures of his life is to spend time soaking in the Word of God: something he does habitually and consistently. He can be compared to a tree whose roots have reached deeply into a fresh stream; a tree which is full of life and bears luscious fruit for others. Yes, this man has a rich and prosperous inner life with God."

4. List the five things which are said of the "wicked" (or sinners) in Psalm 1:4-6.

   Psalm 1:4a (contrast of 1:3)

   Psalm 1:4b

   Psalm 1:5a

   Psalm 1:5b

   Psalm 1:6b

5. The term *chaff* (Heb. *mots*$_{4671}$) is a biblical concept describing those who are empty of substance; whose lives have no value. An interesting contrast is the word "*honor*" (Heb. *kabowd*$_{3519}$), which literally means heavy; it is used in Scripture to describe a man with godly, or weighty, character. Explain the difference in these two terms regarding the righteous and the godless.

Thursday

1. Read and meditate on Psalm 2 (supplemental reading: Ephesians 1).

2. Psalm 2 contains one of the most incredible glimpses provided by Scripture inside the heavenly council. In this short passage, we hear about a mysterious "decree" which has been issued forth regarding the Messiah. This decree (or at least some part of it) is revealed in God's words quoted in Psalm 2:7b-9. Write out what God said to His Son.

3. In eternity past, a decree was issued in the "council of the holy ones," (Psalm 89:7) which encompasses all of God's providential dealings with man. The psalmist states that this is "a decree which will not pass away." (Psalm 148:6) This great and immutable plan was settled before Creation. "My purpose will be established," declares Jehovah, "And I will accomplish all My good pleasure." (Isaiah 46:10)

   Psalm 2 highlights certain aspects of this official edict, *viz.*, that God would establish a kingdom which would be ruled by Messiah—His only begotten Son. This wonderful psalm foretells the Day of the Lord when all things will be brought into subjection to the Christ—"under His feet." (Hebrews 2:8) But Psalm 2 also anticipates man's unwillingness to submit to Christ's authority. Using the following outline as a guide, write out an explanation of this Plan to an unbeliever.

   The Creation of Man
   - His free will
   - His probationary status on earth
   - His eternal destiny

   The Plan of Redemption
   - The foreknowledge of man's rebellion against God's authority
   - A temporary atonement for sin provided by the Law, appropriated through the sacrificial system
   - The first advent of the Messiah and His Kingdom
   - The final atoning work of Calvary appropriated by faith & repentance

   The Second Coming of Christ
   - The conclusion of "man's day"
   - The advent of the "day of the Lord"
   - The subjection of all enemies—demons and men

Thursday - continued

<u>The Judgment</u>

- Eternal damnation of rebels

- The marriage of the Son and His Bride

- Bema Seat Judgment of the redeemed (II Corinthians 5:10)

Friday

1. Read and meditate on Psalm 2 (supplemental reading: II Thessalonians 2).

2. Write out Psalm 2:1-2.

3. Psalm 2:1-2 was a prophecy about the Messiah which was explained by the disciples in Acts 4:25-28. Look up this passage and then explain from memory the story the disciples are referring to.

4. In Psalm 2:3, the psalmist broadens the scope of his prophecy to include all mankind. This verse reveals something about the Lord's dealings with man and man's reaction to it. Explain what you learn about both in this verse.

5. Read what Jesus said in Matthew 11:27-30 and explain in your own words how His statements correspond to the decree mentioned in Psalm 2 and man's reaction to it.

6. In Psalm 2:4-5, we are told that the Lord laughs, scoffs and speaks to rebellious mankind in anger. This is human language describing how man's rebellion leaves God undaunted, for He will judge all rebels in a controlled and systematic manner. What does this say to you regarding God's sovereignty and omnipotence?

7. Read Psalm 2:11 and explain how it is possible to "worship with reverence" and "rejoice with trembling."

1. Read and meditate on Psalm 36 (supplemental reading: Proverbs 1).

2. Read Psalm 36:1-2 in the following translations (and paraphrases) and explain what you learn and how it affects you.

   Psalm 36:1

   (NLT) Sin whispers to the wicked, deep within their hearts. They have no fear of God at all.

   (NET) An evil man is rebellious to the core. He does not fear God,

   (Liv) Sin lurks deep in the hearts of the wicked, forever urging them on to evil deeds. They have no fear of God to hold them back.

   (Har) Rebellion flares up stubbornly in the mind of the wicked; reverence for God has no place in such an outlook.

   Psalm 36:2

   (NIV) For in his own eyes he flatters himself too much to detect or hate his sin.

   (NLT) In their blind conceit, they cannot see how wicked they really are.

   (NET) for he is too proud to recognize and give up his sin.

   (Jer) He sees himself with too flattering an eye to detect and detest his guilt.

3. Review Psalm 1:5-6 and Psalm 2:5, 9 and 12. These verses are primarily describing the judgment of the ungodly. Look up the following verses and explain what you learn about the judgment of the wicked.

   Matthew 25:30

   Matthew 25:41

   Romans 2:4-5, 8-9

   II Thessalonians 1:7b-9

   Hebrews 10:31

   James 2:13

   Revelation 20:11-15

Sunday

1. Read and meditate on Psalms 1 and 2 (supplemental reading: I Samuel 15).

2. There is a great two-fold truth found in Psalm 1:1 that the reader must deal with if he is to enter the deeper life represented in the book of Psalms:

   - The human heart is extremely impressionable to outside influences.
   - You will receive blessings or curses in your life depending, in large part, upon the type of people you allow to influence you.

   Review your homework for Monday and Tuesday and explain how your life in the future will be affected by what you have learned.

3. Reread the paraphrase provided in question 3 in Wednesday's homework. Explain how these blessings may motivate you to spend more time reading, studying and meditating in God's Word.

4. Read the following commentary by Matthew Henry and explain the importance of being submitted to the authority of God in your own life. Also describe the level of your submission to God in your daily life.

   They will be content to entertain such notions of the kingdom of God and the Messiah as will serve them: if the Lord and his anointed will make them rich and great in the world, they will bid them welcome; but if they will restrain their corrupt appetites and passions, regulate and reform their hearts and lives, and bring them under the government of a pure and heavenly religion, truly then *they will not have this man to reign over them,* Luke 19:14. Christ has *bands and cords* for us; those that will be saved by him must be ruled by him. Why do men oppose religion but because they are impatient of its restraints and obligations?[3]

Sunday - *continued*

5. Review your answer to question 7 in Friday's homework. Have you ever worshiped and rejoiced like this? Have you ever witnessed those who have? Write out Psalm 2:11-12 in the first person vernacular (i.e., using I, me, my) as a personalized commitment from yourself to the Lord.

6. In light of what you have learned today, rewrite Ephesians 2:1-3 in your own words, regarding your own past life.

WEEK 2: MY ALL IN ALL

Monday

1. Read and meditate on Psalm 16 (supplemental reading: Revelation 1).

2. Write out Psalm 16:2.

3. Most versions of the Old Testament scriptures substitute the word "Lord" anytime the original language employed God's primary name (pronounced *Yehovah* or *Yahweh* in Hebrew; *Jehovah* in English). In Psalm 16:2, we see the word "Lord" used twice; the actual word in the first occurrence is *Jehovah*, while the second is *Adonai*. Look up the word *Adonai* in a Bible dictionary and describe what you learn.

4. The second phrase in Psalm 16:2 contains one of the richest and most profound realities found in Scripture. One commentator rightly stated, "All the largest desires of the soul have their perfect satisfaction in God."[1] Read the following comments by Roy Hession and describe what you learn.

    The special revelation which this name gives is that of the grace of God. "I am" is an unfinished sentence. It has no object. I am — what? What is our wonder when we discover, as we continue with our Bibles, that He is saying, "I AM whatever My people need" and that the sentence is only left blank that man may bring his many and various needs, as they arise, to complete it!

    Apart from human need this great name of God goes round and round in a closed circle, "I am that I am" — which means that God is incomprehensible. But the moment human need and misery present themselves, He becomes just what that person needs. The verb has at last an object, the sentence is complete and God is revealed and known. Do we lack peace? "I am thy peace," He says. Do we lack strength? "I am thy strength." Do we lack spiritual life? "I am thy life." Do we lack wisdom? "I am thy wisdom", and so on.

    The name "Jehovah" is really like a blank cheque. Your faith can fill in what He is to be to you — just what you need, as each need arises. It is not you, moreover, who are beseeching Him for this privilege, but He who is pressing it upon you. He is asking you to ask. "Hitherto have ye asked nothing in My name: ask, and ye shall receive, that your joy may be full" (John 16:24). Just as water is ever seeking the lowest depths in order to fill them, so is Jehovah ever seeking out man's need in order to satisfy it. Where there is need, there is God. Where there is sorrow, misery, unhappiness, suffering, confusion, folly, oppression, there is the I AM, yearning to turn man's sorrow into bliss whenever man will let Him. It

Monday - continued

is not, therefore, the hungry seeking for bread, but the Bread seeking the hungry; not the sad seeking for joy, but rather Joy seeking the sad; not emptiness seeking fullness, but rather Fullness seeking emptiness. And it is not merely that He supplies our need, but He becomes Himself the fulfillment of our need. He is ever "I am that which My people need."[2]

Tuesday

1. Read and meditate on Psalm 16 (supplemental reading: Deuteronomy 28).

2. Write out Psalm 16:2 in your own words.

3. How would you apply the truth expressed in Psalm 16:2 in our current culture? Do you know of anyone who actually lives his life as though he believes this statement?

4. Psalm 16 contains a list of blessings for those who love God. In your own words, write out what the blessing is in each of the following statements and phrases. (You might need to consult a commentary to grasp the meaning of some of them.)

   Psalm 16:5a

   Psalm 16:5b

   Psalm 16:6

   Psalm 16:7

   Psalm 16:8

   Psalm 16:9a

   Psalm 16:9b

   Psalm 16:10a

   Psalm 16:11a

   Psalm 16:11b

   Psalm 16:11c

Wednesday

1. Read and meditate on Psalm 16 (supplemental reading: Philippians 4).

2. Write out Psalm 16:8.

3. Psalm 16:8 is an expression of the spiritual law of "Cause and Effect." David was not shaken, troubled or anxious in spite of the fact that he was continually in dangerous situations. Explain how he could enjoy this level of peace of mind in such conditions.

4. Read the following commentary on Psalm 16:11 by Albert Barnes and describe what you learn.

> *Is fulness of joy* Not partial joy; not imperfect joy; not joy intermingled with pain and sorrow; not joy which, though in itself real, does not satisfy the desires of the soul, as is the case with much of the happiness which we experience in this life — but joy, full, satisfying, unalloyed, unclouded, unmingled with anything that would diminish its fulness or its brightness; joy that will not be diminished, as all earthly joys must be, by the feeling that it must soon come to an end.[3]

5. Read Psalm 16:5-11 in *The Living Bible* (Liv) and write out what fresh insights or perspectives you gain.

> The Lord himself is my inheritance, my prize. He is my food and drink, my highest joy! He guards all that is mine. He sees that I am given pleasant brooks and meadows as my share! What a wonderful inheritance! I will bless the Lord who counsels me; he gives me wisdom in the night. He tells me what to do. I am always thinking of the Lord; and because he is so near, I never need to stumble or to fall. Heart, body, and soul are filled with joy… You have let me experience the joys of life and the exquisite pleasures of your own eternal presence.

Thursday

1. Read and meditate on Psalm 34 (supplemental reading: Acts 16).

2. Write out Psalm 34:1-2.

3. In Psalm 34:2, David exclaimed, "My soul will make its boast in Jehovah!" Read Jeremiah 9:23-24 and explain what you learn from this passage.

4. The word *boast* (Heb. *halal*$_{1984}$) is often translated as *praise*. Write out the statement or phrase in each of the following verses, replacing the word "praise" with the words "boast in."

    Psalm 22:22b

    Psalm 69:34a

    Psalm 145:2b

    Psalm 146:1

    Psalm 148:2

    Psalm 150:2

    Psalm 150:6

5. Explain how this simple substitution of words affects your perspectives on worship.

Friday

1. Read and meditate on Psalm 34 (supplemental reading: Revelation 14).

2. Write out Psalm 34:7.

3. Look up the following passages about "the angel of the Lord" (skim through the stories) and explain what you learn about these heavenly beings.

   Numbers 22:21-35

   Judges 13:3-21

   I Chronicles 21:11-30

   Isaiah 37:36

   Matthew 2:13-14, 19-21

   Luke 2:8-15

   Acts 12:5-10

4. In light of what you have just learned about "the angel of the Lord," spend a few minutes meditating on what is being expressed in Psalm 34:7. Ask God to open the eyes of your heart so that this will be made real to your soul. Explain what insight you derive through this exercise.

Saturday

1. Read and meditate on Psalm 34 (supplemental reading: Matthew 5).

2. Write out Psalm 34:4 and 6 as one statement in your own words.

3. Read the following verses and write out the blessings indicated in each verse that come to the righteous.

   Psalm 34:9-10

   Psalm 34:15

   Psalm 34:17

   Psalm 34:18

   Psalm 34:22

4. Read the following verses from Psalm 34 in *The Living Bible* (Liv) and write out what fresh insights or perspectives you gain from each.

   Psalm 34:1-2 - "I will praise the Lord no matter what happens. I will constantly speak of his glories and grace. I will boast of all his kindness to me. Let all who are discouraged take heart."

Saturday - continued

Psalm 34:8 - "Oh, put God to the test and see how kind he is! See for yourself the way his mercies shower down on all who trust in him."

Psalm 34:14-15 - "Turn from all known sin and spend your time in doing good. Try to live in peace with everyone; work hard at it. For the eyes of the Lord are intently watching all who live good lives, and he gives attention when they cry to him."

Psalm 34:18-19 - "The Lord is close to those whose hearts are breaking; he rescues those who are humbly sorry for their sins. The good man does not escape all troubles—he has them too. But the Lord helps him in each and every one."

Sunday

1. Read and meditate on Psalm 34 (supplemental reading: Mark 11).

2. Review question 3 in Monday's homework. Can you honestly say that you have actually made God the Lord and Master of your life? Do you wait on Him for direction when you are making important decisions? Have you allowed Him to direct the course of your life or have you pursued your own desires and simply asked Him to bless your plans? Explain your answer.

3. Review questions 2 and 3 in Tuesday's homework. Explain how this verse could apply to your own life.

4. Read the following commentary on Psalm 16:5 by Matthew Henry and honestly evaluate your own life in light of what he expressed. To what degree could this be said about your life? Explain your answer.

> Let me have the love and favour of God, and be accepted of him; let me have the comfort of communion with God, and satisfaction in the communications of his graces and comforts; let me have an interest in his promises, and a title by promise to everlasting life and happiness in the future state; and I have enough, I need no more, I desire no more, to complete my [happiness].[4]

Sunday - *continued*

5. Pick out five verses from Psalm 34 and rewrite them into a personal confession about the Lord.

    a. e.g., verse 5: I looked to God in prayer and He transformed me; He did not mock me or poke fun at my need, but instead provided generously for me.

    b.

    c.

    d.

    e.

WEEK 3 : HE LEADS ME

Monday

1. Read and meditate on Psalm 23 (supplemental reading: II Corinthians 8).

2. Write out Psalm 23:1.

3. Look up the word *want* (Heb. *chacer*$_{2637}$) in a Bible dictionary and list some of the synonyms provided.

   a.   b.

   c.   d.

4. Write out Psalm 23:1 using synonyms provided by your Bible dictionary in place of the word *want*.

   a.   e.g.: The LORD is my shepherd, I shall not *fail*.

   b.

   c.

   d.

5. Look up the following verses and explain what you learn about this word *chaser* and the way the Lord provides for His children.

   Exodus 16:18

Monday - *continued*

Deuteronomy 2:7

Deuteronomy 8:9

Nehemiah 9:21

Psalm 34:10

6. Rewrite Matthew 6:24-34 in your own words in light of what you have just read.

Tuesday

1. Read and meditate on Psalm 23 (supplemental reading: Jeremiah 23).

2. In Psalm 23:2-3, it is said that the Lord does four things for His sheep. Write these out in your own words.

   Psalm 23:2a

   Psalm 23:2b

   Psalm 23:3a

   Psalm 23:3b

3. John 10:1-18 provides a description of the "good shepherd" and also of "thieves and robbers." The good shepherd is primarily Jesus, of course, but the term also represents all ministers who tend His flock. Thieves and robbers are terms that represent false teachers and hirelings; those who enter the sheepfold for selfish purposes. They are takers rather than givers. Look up the following verses and write out what you learn about each.

   Good Shepherd:

   John 10:3

   John 10:4

   John 10:9

   John 10:10b

   John 10:11

   John 10:14

   John 10:16

Tuesday - continued

Thieves:

John 10:1 (Compare with John 10:9)

John 10:5

John 10:10a

John 10:12-13

4. Keeping in mind the contrast you have just seen from John 10, scan the following biblical accounts about conflicts between true and false prophets and explain what you learn. Note those whom the prophets are trying to win to their cause and point out any similarities you see in these stories.

    I Kings 18

    I Kings 22:1-40

    Jeremiah 28

    Acts 15:1-35; Galatians 2:1-10

1. Read and meditate on Psalm 23 (supplemental reading: John 14).

2. Write out Psalm 23:2.

3. Read the following excerpt from a sermon by Alexander MacLaren and describe what you learn.

> It is the hot noontide, and the desert lies baking in the awful glare, and every stone on the hills of Judaea burns the foot that touches it. But in that panting, breathless hour, here is a little green glen, with a quiet brooklet, and moist lush herbage all along its course, and great stones that fling a black shadow over the dewy grass at their base; and there would the shepherd lead his flock…Sweet silence broods there. The sheep feed and drink, and couch in cool lairs till he calls them forth again. So God leads His children…
>
> Thus regarded, the image describes the sweet rest of the soul in communion with God, in whom alone the hungry heart finds food that satisfies, and from whom alone the thirsty soul drinks draughts deep and limpid enough.
>
> This rest and refreshment has for its consequence the restoration of the soul, which includes in it both the invigoration of the natural life by the outward sort of these blessings, and the quickening and restoration of the spiritual life by the inward feeding upon God and repose in Him.[1]

4. Write out Psalm 23:6.

5. Look up the word *follow* (*radaph*[7291]) in a Bible dictionary and write out a short definition for this word.

6. Look up the verses listed below where this same word is used and write out the word or phrase used in your translation.

   a. Deuteronomy 28:45

Wednesday - *continued*

    b. I Samuel 23:25

    c. I Samuel 30:8

    d. Psalm 18:37

    e. Psalm 34:14

    f. Psalm 119:150

    g. Proverbs 11:19

7. In light of what you have just learned, write Psalm 23:6 in your own words.

Thursday

1. Read and meditate on Psalm 25 (supplemental reading: Matthew 7).

2. Write out Psalm 25:4.

3. The words *ways* (Heb. *derek*$_{1870}$) and *paths* (Heb. *'orach*$_{734}$) are two different words. Look both up in a Bible dictionary and provide a concise definition in your own words—a short phrase—for each.

    a. *derek*

    b. *'orach*

4. These two words are used together in a number of biblical passages. Write out the following verses; but replace the terms above with your definition.

    e.g.: Proverbs 2:13 - "From those who leave the *(your definition of 'orach here)* of uprightness to walk in the *(your definition of derek here)* of darkness."

    Psalm 27:11

    Psalm 139:3

    Proverbs 2:20

    Proverbs 3:6

    Proverbs 4:14

    Proverbs 15:19

Friday

1. Read and meditate on Psalm 25 (supplemental reading: Genesis 41).

2. Write out Psalm 25:14.

3. Look up the following verses and explain what you learn about receiving special revelation from the Lord.

   Psalm 119:130

   Proverbs 1:23

   Proverbs 28:5

   Jeremiah 33:3

   Daniel 2:21b-22

   Amos 3:7

   I Corinthians 2:13-14

4. Read the following commentaries on Psalm 25:14 and describe what you learn.

   It is neither learning nor labour that can give insight into God's secrets… These things come by revelation rather than by discourse of reason, and must therefore be obtained by prayer. Those that diligently seek him shall be of his Cabinet Council, shall know his soul secrets, and be admitted into a gracious familiarity and friendship.[2]

   "Find me such a man, and I will tell you how it will fare with him. God will reveal himself to him otherwise than he does to the world. Between them there is sympathy and sweet accord." God opens his mind to those who love him. He lets them into his secrets. They are in the way of light, and evermore, as they advance, the light shines on them more fully…This has been the experience of God's people in all ages. Abraham in his tent (Genesis 18:17), David with his flocks, Daniel in the king's palace, the apostle in the dungeon at Philippi, — all have felt alike that God reveals himself to those who truly serve him.[3]

1. Read and meditate on Psalm 25 (supplemental reading: Daniel 2).

2. Read Psalm 25:14 in the following translations (and paraphrases) and explain what you learn.

    "The secret of the LORD is for those who fear Him, And He will make them know His covenant." (NASB)

    "The LORD confides in those who fear him; he makes his covenant known to them." (NIV)

    "Friendship with God is reserved for those who reverence him. With them alone he shares the secrets of his promises." (Liv)

    "The secret (of the sweet satisfying companionship) of the Lord have they who fear (revere and worship) Him, and He will show them His covenant and reveal to them its (deep, inner) meaning." (AMP)

    "The LORD is the friend of those who obey him and he affirms his covenant with them." (GNB)

3. Read the following commentary from *Albert Barnes* and describe what you learn.

    [The word "secret"] properly means a couch or cushion; and then, a divan or circle of friends sitting together; then, deliberation or consultation; then, familiar contact, intimacy; and then, a "secret," - as if it were the result of a private consultation among friends, or something which pertained to them, and which they did not wish to have known...

    The word "friendship" would perhaps express the meaning here. The sense is, that those who fear the Lord are admitted to the intimacy of friendship with Him; are permitted to come into His presence, and to partake of His counsels; are allowed free access to Him; or, as it is more commonly expressed, have "fellowship" with Him.[4]

4. Write out Psalm 25:8.

5. Look up Luke 7:34 and compare it to the story found in Matthew 9:9-13. What similarities do you see in what was said about Jesus and what David said about God in Psalm 25:8?

Sunday

1. Read and meditate on Psalm 23 (supplemental reading: Acts 8).

2. Write out Psalm 25:5.

3. Compare Luke 4:1 with Romans 8:14 and explain what it means to be led by the Spirit. If someone were to challenge your faith in Christ, could you honestly articulate how you are led by the Spirit? Explain your answer.

4. Fanny Crosby, the great songwriter of the 19th Century, lived nearly her entire life in blindness. Her song "All the Way My Savior Leads Me" takes on special significance when one thinks of a blind person being led around by the hand. Take your time and meditate on the words she penned so long ago. Write out any revelations that come to you through this.

   All the way my Savior leads me; What have I to ask beside? Can I doubt His tender mercy, Who thro' life has been my guide? Heav'nly peace, divinest comfort, Here by faith in Him to dwell! For I know whate'er befall me, Jesus doeth all things well; For I know whate'er befall me, Jesus doeth all things well.

   All the way my Savior leads me; Cheers each winding path I tread, Gives me grace for ev'ry trial, Feeds me with the living bread; Tho' my weary steps may falter, And my soul athirst may be, Gushing from the Rock before me, Lo! A spring of joy I see; Gushing from the Rock before me, Lo! A spring of joy I see.

   All the way my Savior leads me; Oh, the fullness of His love! Perfect rest to me is promised In my Father's house above; When my spirit, clothed immortal, Wings its flight to realms of day, This my song thro' endless ages: Jesus led me all the way; This my song thro' endless ages: Jesus led me all the way.[5]

WEEK 4 : BATTLING ENEMIES

Monday

1. Read and meditate on Psalm 7 (supplemental reading: I Samuel 18).

2. Write out Psalm 7:9.

3. Within the 150 Psalms, most of which were penned by David, there are certain passages or even entire psalms where the writer calls upon God to destroy his enemies. These are called "Imprecatory Psalms," and they must be understood in light of the period in which they were written. Read the following explanation by Charles Ryrie and explain what you learn.

    These psalms (7, 35, 55, 58, 59, 69, 79, 109, 137, 139), which invoke judgment or curses on one's enemies perplex many. Consider, however, that the purposes of these imprecations are (1) to demonstrate God's just and righteous judgment toward the wicked (58:11); (2) to show the authority of God over the wicked (59:13); (3) to lead the wicked to seek the Lord (83:16); (4) to cause the righteous to praise God (7:17). Therefore, out of zeal for God and abhorrence of sin, the psalmist calls on God to punish the wicked and to vindicate His righteousness.[1]

4. Look up the following verses which Charles Ryrie referred to and explain in your own words what you learn, especially in light of what you just read.

    Psalm 58:11

    Psalm 59:13

    Psalm 83:16

    Psalm 7:17

Tuesday

1. Read and meditate on Psalm 35:1-23 (supplemental reading: I Samuel 22).

2. Write out Psalm 35:5-6 in your own words.

3. Read the following commentary by Charles Spurgeon and describe what you learn about the terrible fate of God's enemies.

> When this imprecation is fulfilled in graceless men, they will find it an awful thing to be for ever without rest, without peace of mind, or stay of soul, hurried from fear to fear, and from misery to misery. *"And let the angel of the Lord chase them."* Fallen angels shall haunt them, good angels shall afflict them. To be pursued by avenging spirits will be the lot of those who delight in persecution. Observe the whole scene as the Psalmist sketches it: the furious foe is first held at bay, then turned back, then driven to headlong flight, and chased by fiery messengers from whom there is no escape, while his pathway becomes dark and dangerous, and his destruction overwhelming.
>
> *"Let their way be dark and slippery."* What terrors are gathered here! No light, no foothold, and a fierce avenger at their heels! What a doom is appointed for the enemies of God! They may rage and rave today, but how altered will be their plight ere long! *"And let the angel of the Lord persecute them."* He will follow them hot-foot, as we say, never turning aside, but like a trusty pursuivant serving the writ of vengeance upon them, and arresting them in the name of unflinching justice. Woe, woe, woe, unto those who touch the people of God; their destruction is both swift and sure.[2]

4. One of the primary differences between the periods of the Old and New Testaments is that the emphasis shifted from the outward, visible life to the inward life. For instance, much of David's life was spent in physical, hand-to-hand combat with his foes. When he thought of his enemies, he could envision soldiers of neighboring nations or even the faces of treacherous men in his own country. At that point, very little was known about the invisible forces which were hostile to God's kingdom. The New Testament brought about a greater awareness of the unseen realm around us. Christians understand that their real enemy is not man but the demonic forces which are opposed to God. Look up the following verses and explain in your own words what you learn about God's enemies.

Job 2:1-2

Tuesday - continued

Daniel 10:12-13

Matthew 12:22

Luke 8:27-34

II Corinthians 2:11

II Corinthians 10:3-5

II Corinthians 11:3

II Corinthians 11:14

Ephesians 6:12

Wednesday

1. Read and meditate on Psalm 55:1-8 (supplemental reading: Ephesians 6).

2. Write out Psalm 55:3 in your own words with our present day enemies in mind.

3. Look up the following verses about David's foes. Consider the real enemies who were inciting and encouraging their hatred of him. Write out each verse(s) in your own words, using terms such as "demons" or "evil spirits" to describe his adversaries.

    Psalm 31:13

    Psalm 56:5-6

    Psalm 64:2-3

    Psalm 109:2-3

    Psalm 140:2-3

4. In Psalm 5:9 David offers a deeper description of the "voice of the enemy." Read this verse in the following translations (and paraphrases) and explain what you learn about the thoughts which demons sometimes implant into our minds.

    "There is nothing reliable in what they say; their inward part is destruction itself. Their throat is an open grave; they flatter with their tongue." (NASB)

Wednesday - continued

"For they cannot speak one truthful word. Their hearts are filled to the brim with wickedness. Their suggestions are full of the stench of sin and death. Their tongues are filled with flatteries to gain their wicked ends." (Liv)

"For there is nothing trustworthy or steadfast or truthful in their talk; their heart is destruction [*or a destructive chasm, a yawning gulf*]; their throat is an open sepulcher; they flatter and make smooth with their tongue." (AMP)

"For no faith may be put in their words; their inner part is nothing but evil; their throat is like an open place for the dead; smooth are the words of their tongues." (BBE)

"What my enemies say can never be trusted; they only want to destroy. Their words are flattering and smooth, but full of deadly deceit." (GNB)

"My enemies cannot speak a truthful word. Their deepest desire is to destroy others. Their talk is foul, like the stench from an open grave. Their tongues are filled with flattery." (NLT)

Wednesday - continued

Thursday

1. Read and meditate on Psalm 55:9-23 (supplemental reading: II Samuel 15).

2. Write out Psalm 55:9 in your own words with our present day enemies in mind.

3. Most commentators believe that Psalm 55 was written by David when his friend Ahithophel joined Absalom's revolt against him and he had to flee for his life. Compare David's prayer in Psalm 55:9, 12-15 with his prayer in II Samuel 15:31. Then read the account of how his prayer was answered in II Samuel 18:1-15. Explain what you learn from this regarding how to silence the voice of the enemy.

4. Some teachers underestimate the role the devil and demons play in the temptation of believers. Look up the following verses and explain what you learn about how the enemy operates in the realm of our minds.

    I Chronicles 21:1

    Matthew 4:3

    Matthew 16:21-23

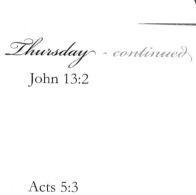

Thursday - continued

John 13:2

Acts 5:3

Ephesians 6:11

James 4:6b-7

I Peter 5:8-9

Revelation 13:11-15

Friday

1. Read and meditate on Psalm 59 (supplemental reading: I Samuel 19).

2. Write out Psalm 59:1.

3. Psalm 59 is an expression of what David experienced when some of Saul's henchmen attempted to murder him. David escaped, but according to Psalm 59:1, to whom did he look for his deliverance?

4. Jehoshaphat faced a similar danger himself. Read the account of what happened in II Chronicles 20:1-24 and answer the following questions.

   a. According to II Chronicles 20:1-3a, what was Jehoshaphat's initial reaction to the news of the invading armies?

   b. According to II Chronicles 20:3b-4, what two things did Jehoshaphat call upon the people of Judah to do in response to this threat?

5. II Chronicles 20:6-12 contains the gist of Jehoshaphat's prayer to the Lord about the impending threat they faced. List five things Jehoshaphat reminded the Lord about in II Chronicles 20:6-10.

   a.

   b.

   c.

   d.

   e.

Friday - continued

6. According to II Chronicles 20:12, how did Jehoshaphat compare Judah's ability to win this war with the Lord's?

7. According to II Chronicles 20:14-17, what did the Lord do to comfort Jehoshaphat and his people?

8. According to II Chronicles 20:18, what was their response to what they heard?

9. According to II Chronicles 20:21, what did Jehoshaphat do to pave the way for victory in this battle?

10. According to II Chronicles 20:22-24, what was the outcome of putting their trust in Jehovah?

11. List three benefits found in II Chronicles 20:25-30 which the people of Judah experienced because of going through this trial.

    a.

    b.

    c.

Saturday

1. Read and meditate on Psalm 69 (supplemental reading: Daniel 10).

2. There are three phrases in Psalm 69:4. Keeping with the idea of demonic forces being our real enemies, write out the first two phrases in your own words.

   a.

   b.

3. Use terminology from the following passages of Scripture to create four "spiritual warfare" prayers which you can use in the future: Psalm 3; Psalm 17:6-13; Psalm 21:8-13; Psalm 31:13-18; Psalm 54; Psalm 56:1-9; Psalm 68:1-4.

   a.

   b.

   c.

   d.

Sunday

1. Read and meditate on Psalm 58 (supplemental reading: Psalm 150).

2. Write out Psalm 58:3b-4a.

3. A couple of years ago my wife and I were counseling Phil and Judy, a couple who had come to us seeking help. One of the issues that came out during our counseling sessions with them was that Judy's unsaved mother hated Phil and would use every opportunity to malign his character to Judy. It was clear to us that the enemy was using the mother-in-law to poison Judy's attitude toward her husband. We did our utmost to convince her that she should believe the best about her husband and become supportive of him. When she spent time around us, her attitude toward him would soften. But every time she visited her mother, she became suspicious and critical of Phil. In the end, she came to recognize how the devil was using her mother to destroy her marriage. She had a straightforward talk with her mother, telling her that, in the future, if she began to badmouth Phil, she would have no other choice but to leave. Once she followed up on her threats a couple of times, the accusations came to an end.

    Can you think of anyone the enemy has used to poison your mind toward someone else? Explain what happened and the outcome.

4. The Christian who tolerates ungodly messages will find himself becoming increasingly more open to a darker and more evil message. He is becoming desensitized to the subtle inroads of the enemy. Perhaps without realizing it, he is gradually losing his resistance to evil. What television programs do you regularly watch that present evil messages or situations? How do you think this affects your spiritual life? Explain your answer.

Sunday - continued

5. Briefly review the story of Jehoshaphat found in Friday's homework. Read the following passage from *At the Altar of Sexual Idolatry* and describe what you learn about how true worship can affect the spiritual atmosphere around you. Do you ever spend time in heartfelt praise to God? Can you see how it might be a benefit to your spiritual life? Explain your answer.

Something very powerful occurs in the spiritual realm when a person begins truly praising God. Heart-felt praise cleans out the atmosphere of demonic activity. I remember standing in chapel service while in Bible college once. We spent time singing every morning, but this particular day we seemed to enter into a higher level of worship. As I closed my eyes, a picture formed in my mind. High above us was the presence of a holy God, and between the students and the Lord was a thick cloud of satanic darkness. This evil presence was keeping us from Him, but as we lifted up our voices in praise, that ugly cloud separated and soon dissipated. Our praise opened up a direct avenue to God![3]

WEEK 5 : THE LOVINGKINDNESS OF THE LORD

Monday

1. Read and meditate on Psalm 118:1-14 (supplemental reading: Exodus 14).

2. Write out Psalm 118:1.

3. The lovingkindness (i.e., *mercy*) of the Lord is mentioned 127 times in the book of Psalms and is clearly one of its most prominent themes. Read the following passage from my book *Living in Victory* and describe what you learn about it.

   Mercy is living out the love of God. The Old Testament Hebrew word translated mercy in the King James Bible is *hhesed*. It is translated as "lovingkindness" in the NASB and "unfailing love" in the NIV. Hhesed primarily refers to the supply system God established on this earth to meet needs: physical, emotional, and spiritual. In short, mercy is love in action. Grace is the welcoming smile of God. Compassion is the natural response of God toward needs. Mercy is the provision for that need.[1]

4. Look up the following verses and explain what you learn about God's mercy.

   Deuteronomy 7:9

   I Kings 8:23

   Psalm 25:10

Monday - continued

Psalm 86:5

Psalm 145:8

Psalm 145:9

Ephesians 2:3-5

Tuesday

1. Read and meditate on Psalm 104 (supplemental reading: Jeremiah 31).

2. Write out Psalm 33:4b and Psalm 33:5b in your own words as a single sentence.

3. Read Psalm 33:5b in the following translations (and paraphrases) and write out a statement of your own which encompasses the various thoughts presented.

   "The earth is full of the mercy of the Lord." (BBE)

   "The earth is filled with his tender love." (Liv)

   "The earth is full of divine blessing." (Har)

   "Yahweh's love fills the earth." (Jer)

4. Review Psalm 104 and write out 15 things the Lord did to provide for the needs of His creation.

   a.

   b.

   c.

   d.

   e.

Tuesday - continued

f.

g.

h.

i.

j.

k.

l.

m.

n.

o.

Wednesday

1. Read and meditate on Psalm 72 (supplemental reading: Hosea 2).

2. Write out Psalm 72:12.

3. Look up the following verses and explain what you learn about those who see their need for God's mercy.

   Psalm 10:17-18

   Psalm 68:5-6

   Psalm 72:12-14

   Psalm 102:17, 20

   Psalm 113:7-9

4. Read the following passage from *Living in Victory* and describe what you learn about God's willingness to help those who see their need.

   We all have deep emotional and spiritual needs that can only be met by God and through Him alone. The wonderful news is that God has a universe full of mercy for all of us—mercy to meet our needs, to set us free, and to heal our infirmities, allowing each of us to enter into a life of blessedness. The allocation of this need-fulfilling mercy comes once we begin to see our need for it. The only hindrance to receiving such unmerited favor from Him hinges upon how much we choose to appropriate for ourselves…

   If Bartimaeus were not blind, would he have been bellowing unashamedly, "Son of David, have mercy on me!" (Mark 10:47)? If the Syro-Phoenician woman's daughter had not been vexed with a devil would she have been willing to "eat of the crumbs which fall from their masters' table" (Matthew 15:27 KJV)? Had King David not been sharply rebuked by

Wednesday ~ *continued*

Nathan and been forced to see his great crime, would he have ever penned the words, "Have mercy upon me, O God, according to thy lovingkindness: according unto the multitude of thy tender mercies blot out my transgressions" (Psalm 51:1 KJV)? Had Peter not seen how unlike the Lord he was, would he have cried out, "Depart from me, for I am a sinful man, O Lord!" (Luke 5:8)? And finally, if the publican had not seen his great need, would he have "smote upon his breast, saying, 'God be merciful to me a sinner'" (Luke 18:13 KJV)?[2]

Thursday

1. Read and meditate on Psalm 107 (supplemental reading: Isaiah 48).

2. Write out Psalm 107:43 in your own words.

3. The word lovingkindness is used six times in Psalm 107. According to Psalm 107:2, what are the "redeemed" commanded to say?

4. Psalm 107 offers four different pictures of those who needed God's mercy in their lives. Carefully study the dynamics of these different groups of people in each of these passages and explain what you learn. Take note of what brought them to see their need for His help, what they did about it and what He did for them.

    Psalm 107:4-9

    Psalm 107:10-16

    Psalm 107:17-22

    Psalm 107:23-32

5. Can you think of any biblical characters who the Lord, in His mercy, attempted to rescue from their own folly? Briefly tell the story.

Friday

1. Read and meditate on Psalm 112 (supplemental reading: Romans 12).

2. Write out Psalm 41:1

3. Write out Matthew 10:8 in your own words and explain the general principle the Lord was teaching in this statement.

4. Review Psalm 112:5-9 and list seven benefits for the merciful man.

    a.

    b.

    c.

    d.

    e.

    f.

    g.

5. Read Luke 6:27-38 and explain what you think the Lord meant in verse 38.

6. James summed up Christianity in one poignant statement. Look up James 1:27 and describe in your own words what the true Christian life looks like.

Saturday

1. Read and meditate on Psalm 136 (supplemental reading: Isaiah 53).

2. Write out Psalm 109:4-5 in your own words.

3. There is no question that David was a fierce warrior, but he was also a man of lovingkindness. Read Psalm 35:12-15 and explain what you learn about how David treated those who later turned against him.

4. Exodus 32 recounts the story of the children of Israel worshiping the golden calf and God's reaction to it. Read Exodus 32:9-14 and describe how Moses was used by the Lord to rescue the rebels.

5. There is no question that God blesses those who live out His love to other people. But His blessings are often intangible benefits such as the inner joy of operating in His love. The fact of the matter is that there is also a price to pay when you begin to meet the needs of other people. Read the following passage from *Living in Victory* and describe what you learn about the sacrifice involved in living out God's love to others.

> There is a very good reason why John spoke of believers laying down their lives for each other, and why Paul spoke of being poured out as a drink offering. A person who loves others and does for others, makes himself vulnerable. When you care about people, you often get hurt. People turn on you, they lie about you, they use you, they steal from you, and they disappoint you. All of this is part and parcel for any real work of God. There are hardships sure to be faced to one degree or another for anybody living the mercy life…
>
> Suffering loss, sacrificing for others, feeling the stinging criticisms of detractors, being used by those you are trying to help, having things go wrong that shouldn't, and being hurt by those you are called to love are all part of living the mercy life. And yet, in some strange way, it is also part of the glory of the high calling. Christians are soldiers and their medals of valor are the scars they have suffered for their Savior.[3]

Sunday

1. Read and meditate on Psalm 136 (supplemental reading: Matthew 9).

2. Write out Luke 6:32.

3. Review the passage from *Living in Victory* found in the third question of Monday's homework. Write out each of the last three sentences in the spaces below, along with an explanation about how they have been true in your own personal life. Give examples.

    a.

    b.

    c.

3. Review your answers to the fourth question of Thursday's homework. Can you relate to any of these scenarios in your own life? Which one seems most applicable? Explain your answer.

4. Review Friday's homework. How are you involved in meeting the needs of other people? Give concrete examples of how the Lord is living out His love through you to others.

WEEK 6: MY KEEPER AND REFUGE

Monday

1. Read and meditate on Psalm 121 (supplemental reading: Matthew 2).

2. Write out Psalm 121:3.

3. Look up the word *keeps* (Heb. *shamar*$_{8104}$) in a Bible dictionary and list some of the synonyms provided.

   a.   b.

   c.   d.

4. This Hebrew term is used 6 different times in this short psalm to show what the Lord does for His elect. Explain in your own words what you learn in each of the following phrases.

   Psalm 121:3b

   Psalm 121:4

   Psalm 121:5-6

   Psalm 121:7a

   Psalm 121:7b

   Psalm 121:8

Monday - *continued*

3. Look up the following verses and explain what else you learn about how the Lord keeps His children.

Psalm 37:28

Psalm 41:2

Psalm 91:11

Psalm 127:1b

Psalm 145:20a

Tuesday

1. Read and meditate on Psalm 119:55-67 (supplemental reading: Proverbs 7).

2. Write out Psalm 119:9.

3. The Hebrew word *shamar* is also used regarding the spiritual responsibilities of God's people. Look up the following verses and explain what you learn.

   Psalm 17:4

   Psalm 18:21

   Psalm 18:23

   Psalm 37:34

   Psalm 39:1

   Psalm 106:3

Tuesday - *continued*

4. Read Psalm 107:43 and the following commentary by Rex Andrews and describe what you learn.

> The wise here mentioned are those who observe the things found in this Psalm. If they keep these things, preserve them, attend to them, then they shall understand the lovingkindness of the Lord. It is wisdom to understand God's mercy-lovingkindness… There is a fallacy about much hearing. It is that one may deceive himself that having heard, he knows. Knowledge comes by doing, experiencing what we hear. The Bible teaches in many places and many ways that lesson. The knowledge of God is found in His mercy—doing it, living it. For mercy, lovingkindness, is what Love DOES.[1]

Wednesday

1. Read and meditate on Psalm 62 (supplemental reading: II Kings 18).

2. Write out Psalm 62:1.

3. Read through the following translations (and paraphrases) of Psalm 62:1 and explain what you learn about the connection between silently waiting upon God and putting your trust in Him.

   "FOR GOD alone my soul waits in silence; from Him comes my salvation." (AMP)

   "I wait patiently for God to save me; I depend on him alone." (GNB)

   "I wait quietly before God, for my victory comes from him." (NLT)

   "Truly my soul looks in stillness to God." (Ber)

   "Only in God is my soul quieted." (ABPS)

4. Solomon rightly said that there is "a time to be silent and a time to speak." (Ecclesiastes 3:7b) Look up the following verses and explain what you learn about those times when silence is called for.

   Exodus 14:14

   Lamentations 3:26

   Habakkuk 2:20

Wednesday - continued

Zephaniah 1:7a

Revelation 8:1

5. Read and meditate on Psalm 62:5-8. In your own words, write out these four verses as a statement of trust in God.

Thursday

1. Read and meditate on Psalm 91 (supplemental reading: John 15)

2. Write out Psalm 91:1.

3. Psalm 91 is a series of conditional promises. It lays out marvelous benefits for those to whom they apply. Write out in your own words the four conditions attached to these blessings.

   Psalm 91:1

   Psalm 91:9

   Psalm 91:14a

   Psalm 91:14b

4. Read the following commentary by Charles Spurgeon and describe what you learn.

   The blessings here promised are not for all believers, but for those who live in close fellowship with God. Every child of God looks towards the inner sanctuary and the mercy seat, yet all do not dwell in the most holy place; they run to it at times, and enjoy occasional approaches, but they do not habitually reside in the mysterious presence.

   Those who through rich grace obtain unusual and continuous communion with God, so as to abide in Christ and Christ in them, become possessors of rare and special benefits, which are missed by those who follow afar off, and grieve the Holy Spirit of God. Into the secret place those only come who know the love of God in Christ Jesus, and those only dwell there to whom to live is Christ.

   Elect out of the elect, they have "attained unto the first three", and shall walk with their Lord in white, for they are worthy… Special grace like theirs brings with it special immunity. Outer court worshippers little know what belongs to the inner sanctuary, or surely they would press on until the place of nearness and divine familiarity became theirs. Those who are the Lord's constant guests shall find that he will never suffer any to be injured within his gates; he has eaten the covenant salt with them, and is pledged for their protection.[2]

Friday

1. Read and meditate on Psalm 91 (supplemental reading: Isaiah 24-27).

2. Write out Psalm 91:7 in your own words.

3. In Isaiah 24-27, a prophecy is given of a great storm which will sweep across the world prior to the return of Christ. The imagery of a storm is very illuminating. Thunderstorms tend to move with unrelenting purpose into an area. The sky becomes increasingly dark. Before long, flashes of lightning begin to burst across the black sky. When it is a storm cell, a great, churning power is at work within the system that can spawn tornadoes.

    This is truly a picture of how the Lord operates. God is unrelenting in accomplishing His purposes. In His sovereign will, He often allows storms of calamity to move into a nation or even continent. When the disaster has passed, many of the wicked have been destroyed, while the righteous have been refined.

    Scan Isaiah 24-27 to get a sense about what has been foretold, paying special attention to Isaiah 26:1-4. Can you see how the Lord can keep you through the most overwhelming adversities? Explain your answer.

4. In Isaiah 25:4, we are told that the Lord is "a defense for the needy in his distress, a refuge from the storm…" Prior to the worldwide storm that was unleashed during Noah's time, anyone who was willing to repent and put his faith in God would have been welcomed into the ark. Some teachers see a comparison of the Flood to the end times. They believe that Jesus Himself will be the "ark" that will take His people through the tribulation period. Review Psalm 91 and give a detailed explanation about how this psalm is a promise of refuge for those who love God.

Saturday

1. Read and meditate on Psalm 91 (supplemental reading: Ezekiel 9).

2. Write out Psalm 91:14.

3. Read Psalm 91 and list ten promises that are made to the believer who trusts and loves God.

    a.

    b.

    c.

    d.

    e.

    f.

    g.

    h.

    i.

    j.

4. Read Psalm 91:1-6 from *The Psalms for Today* (Har) and explain what you learn and how it affects you.

    He who lives as a ward of the Most High shall repose under the protection of the Almighty. I will say of the Lord, "You are my sheltering haven; my God whom I trust."… He will safeguard you with His strength, and you will find shelter within His protecting power; His fidelity is your assurance of security. You will not need to be afraid of any nocturnal terror, nor of any danger that is abroad in daylight. Neither the plague that stalks at dead of night, nor the epidemic which devastates at midday.

Sunday

1. Read and meditate on Psalm 91 (supplemental reading: I Samuel 23).

2. Look up the following prayers of the psalmist and rewrite them in your own words as a prayer to God.

   Psalm 16:1

   Psalm 17:8

   Psalm 25:20

   Psalm 86:2

   Psalm 140:4

   Psalm 141:9

3. Look up the following declarations of the psalmist and rewrite them in your own words to the Lord.

   Psalm 119:17

   Psalm 119:34

   Psalm 119:88

   Psalm 119:101

   Psalm 119:167

   Psalm 119:168

WEEK 7: IN SEARCH OF YAHWEH

Monday

1. Read and meditate on Psalm 27:7-14 (supplemental reading: I Samuel 9).

2. Write out Psalm 27:8.

3. There are three words in the Hebrew language which are translated as *seek*. Look up the word *seek* (Heb. *baqash*[1245]) in a Bible dictionary and list six synonyms provided.

   a.   b.

   c.   d.

   e.   f.

4. Write out Psalm 27:8 using each of the synonyms you listed above in place of the word *seek*.

   a.   e.g.: When You said, "*Search for* My face," my heart said to You, "Your face, O LORD, I shall *search for*."

   b.

   c.

   d.

   e.

   f.

Monday - continued

5. Look up Genesis 37:16 and I Samuel 9:3 where you will find two different stories related to those who are searching "high and low" for something (or someone). Now look up Deuteronomy 4:29 and explain it in light of these two stories.

6. Notice in Psalm 27:7-8 that David had been crying out to the Lord and then those wonderful words were whispered to his soul: "Seek My face." Read the following excerpt from the *Pulpit Commentary* and describe what you learn.

> "Seek, and ye shall find," is one of the great laws of life. The miner must dig for the precious ore; the fishermen must launch out into the deep, and let down his nets for a draught; the husbandman must plough and sow and have long patience, if he is to reap. How is it that in these days the secrets of nature have been laid bare as never before? Because men have sought as they never sought before. And why, in the midst of these discoveries, have so many keen eyes failed to find God? Because they have not sought.[1]

Tuesday

1. Read and meditate on Psalm 105 (supplemental reading: Exodus 33).

2. Write out Psalm 105:3-4.

3. The word *face* used in Psalm 105:4 (Heb. *paniym*$_{6440}$) is often translated as *presence* or "*before* the Lord." With this in mind, look up the following verses and explain what you learn about the *paniym* of God.

    Genesis 3:8

    Genesis 18:22

    Exodus 33:11, 14-15

    Exodus 33:20

    Deuteronomy 9:18

    I Samuel 1:15

    Psalm 11:7

    Psalm 13:1

    Psalm 16:11

    Psalm 51:11

    Psalm 80:19

Wednesday

1. Read and meditate on Psalm 24 (supplemental reading: II Peter 1).

2. Write out Psalm 24:6.

3. Look up the word *seek* (Heb. *darash*$_{1875}$) in a Bible dictionary and describe what you learn.

4. Look up Deuteronomy 19:18 where this term is used to describe a thorough investigation of a false witness. With this usage in mind, look up the following verses and explain what you learn about seeking the Lord.

   I Chronicles 16:11

   II Chronicles 12:14

   II Chronicles 15:12-13

   Psalm 9:10

   Psalm 10:4

   Psalm 34:4

   Psalm 34:10

Wednesday - *continued*

Psalm 111:2

Isaiah 55:6

Lamentations 3:25

5. Pick out four of the verses listed above and write them out, replacing the word *seek* with the phrase *do a thorough investigation of* (using the proper tense required by the sentence structure).

   a. e.g.: Psalm 34:10: The young lions do lack and suffer hunger; but they who *do a thorough investigation of* the LORD shall not be in want of any good thing.

   b.

   c.

   d.

Wednesday - *continued*

Thursday

1. Read and meditate on Psalm 14 (supplemental reading: II Chronicles 15)

2. Write out Psalm 14:2.

3. In Psalm 78:32-35, the psalmist recounts God's dealings with the children of Israel in the wilderness. Read this passage and explain what had to happen to create enough interest in their hearts to seek God.

4. Read the following passage, written by A.W. Tozer, bemoaning the apathy of our age and describe what you learn.

> In the midst of this great chill there are some, I rejoice to acknowledge, who will not be content with shallow logic. They will admit the force of the argument [that seeking God is only for spiritual teachers], and then turn away with tears to hunt some lonely place and pray, "O God, show me thy glory." They want to taste, to touch with their hearts, to see with their inner eyes the wonder that is God.
>
> I want deliberately to encourage this mighty longing after God. The lack of it has brought us to our present low estate. The stiff and wooden quality about our religious lives is a result of our lack of holy desire. Complacency is a deadly foe of all spiritual growth. Acute desire must be present or there will be no manifestation of Christ to His people. He waits to be wanted. Too bad that with many of us He waits so long, so very long, in vain.
>
> Every age has its own characteristics. Right now we are in an age of religious complexity. The simplicity which is in Christ is rarely found among us. In its stead are programs, methods, organizations and a world of nervous activities which occupy time and attention but can never satisfy the longing of the heart. The shallowness of our inner experience, the hollowness of our worship, and that servile imitation of the world which marks our promotional methods all testify that we, in this day, know God only imperfectly, and the peace of God scarcely at all.[2]

Thursday - *continued*

5. Pick out three sentences or phrases written by Mr. Tozer above that you consider to be exceptional and explain what they mean to you.

    a.

    b.

    c.

Thursday - *continued*

Friday

1. Read and meditate on Psalm 63 (supplemental reading: Isaiah 55).

2. Write out Psalm 63:1.

3. Look up the word *seek* (Heb. *shachar*7836) in a Bible dictionary and describe what you learn.

4. The great contrast of rising early to seek the face of God is staying up late to indulge in the frivolity of the world. Read the following excerpts from an article written by this author and describe what you learn.

> This world is a dry and weary land. Nothing will deaden a person's spiritual appetite like the spirit of this world. Even believers with the best of intentions find that their passion for God wanes in the spiritually polluted atmosphere around us. And the more immersed we become in it, the more dry and weary become our souls. Every minute we spend watching television, listening to secular radio, surfing the Net, playing video games, reading newspapers & magazines, strolling through the mall—and a thousand other activities which beckon us—the more barren we become spiritually.
>
> Most believers understand from past experience that the more time they spend in worldly activities, the more difficult it will be to break into the presence of God during their devotions the following morning. They will have to fight through that fog Jesus called "dissipation:" the spiritual hangover that comes from being drunk with the things of this world. It is simply a fact that the world deadens spiritual sensitivity.
>
> One would think that spending time in the world would create a great thirst for the rivers of life, but actually it has the very opposite effect. The things of this world give a person a false sense of fulfillment. It's like filling up on soda pop when the body needs pure water.
>
> The believer who thirsts for God – like a deer pants for streams of water – limits his time in this world. He rises early and cries out, "O God, Thou art my God!" There is a thirst for God and the things of God that cannot be quenched. He longs for "the Fountain of Living Waters," and refuses to drink from the "broken cisterns" of this world.[3]

1. Read and meditate on Psalm 63 (supplemental reading: John 4).

2. Write out Psalm 63:8.

3. Read the following passage about this verse from the *Pulpit Commentary* and describe what you learn.

> There is mutual action. The soul cleaves to God, and God cleaves to the soul. There is a double embrace — we both hold and are upheld. The result is invigoration — the quickening glow of life through all our being, the free and joyous resolve to cleave to God, and to follow him in love and devotion all our days. Our needs are constant, and God's love never fails. When we are weak, his strength makes us strong; when we are weary, his comforts sustain our fainting souls; when we are ready to sink in the waters, his voice gives us courage, and his strong arm brings us salvation. God ever comes to those who want him. Desire on our part is met by satisfaction on his part. More and more as we love and serve we enter into the joy of our Lord.[4]

4. Read Psalm 63:1-8 in *The Good News Bible* (GNB) and write out what fresh insights or perspectives you gain.

> O God, you are my God, and I long for you. My whole being desires you; like a dry, worn-out, and waterless land, my soul is thirsty for you. Let me see you in the sanctuary; let me see how mighty and glorious you are. Your constant love is better than life itself, and so I will praise you. I will give you thanks as long as I live; I will raise my hands to you in prayer. My soul will feast and be satisfied, and I will sing glad songs of praise to you. As I lie in bed, I remember you; all night long I think of you, because you have always been my help. In the shadow of your wings I sing for joy. I cling to you, and your hand keeps me safe.

Saturday - *continued*

5. Write out eight action statements or phrases from the passage above.

a. e.g.: I will raise my hands to you in prayer.

b.

c.

d.

e.

f.

g.

h.

i.

Sunday

1. Read and meditate on Psalm 63 (supplemental reading: Ephesians 3).

2. Review Monday's homework. Explain how often and in what ways you "search for" God. Perhaps this would be a good opportunity to write out a commitment to the Lord to be more diligent about this spiritual exercise.

3. Write out Philippians 3:8, 10 and 12.

4. Compare what you discovered in Wednesday's homework with these verses in Philippians. Explain any comparisons that you see in the concepts presented in each.

5. Review Mr. Tozer's comments in Thursday's homework. How does your Christian life line up with what he is describing? To what degree would you consider yourself to be a sincere and earnest seeker of God? Explain your answers.

Sunday - *continued*

6. Review the author's article in Friday's homework. How much time do you spend soaking in the world's atmosphere? Note any specific changes you are being led to make.

WEEK 8: A DWELLING PLACE OF GOD

Monday

1. Read and meditate on Psalm 84 (supplemental reading: Numbers 16).

2. Write out Psalm 84:1-2.

3. To understand this marvelous psalm, a quick review of the history of the Israelites is in order. If you recall, Moses was of the tribe of Levi. When the children of Israel worshiped the golden calf while Moses was with God on Mt. Sinai, it was his fellow Levites who slew 3,000 participants in the orgy. Because they had acted as defenders of God's righteousness, He appointed them as perpetual guardians of the tabernacle. (Numbers 1:51; 18:22-23a; Deuteronomy 10:8; I Chronicles 6:48; etc.)

   Some time later, Korah, who was one of the leaders of the tribe, rose up in rebellion to the authority God had invested in Moses. He and a number of his followers were subsequently destroyed. Nevertheless, his descendents became known for their adoration of Jehovah and their dedication to His Temple. Eleven psalms are ascribed to the "sons of Korah."

   In Psalm 84, for some unknown reason (e.g., imprisonment, exile, sickness) the author has found himself unable to return to his service in the Temple. It is obvious from what he expresses in this psalm that he is fondly recalling the wonderful experiences he had in the tabernacle of the Lord and is longing to return there. Read the following commentary by Matthew Henry and describe what you learn.

   > It was an entire desire; body, soul, and spirit concurred in it. He was not conscious to himself of any rising thought to the contrary. It was an intense desire; it was like the desire of the ambitious, or covetous, or voluptuous. He longed, he fainted, he cried out, importunate to be restored to his place in God's courts, and almost impatient of delay. Yet it was not so much the courts of the Lord that he coveted, but he cried out, in prayer, *for the living God* himself. O that I might know him, and be again taken into communion with him![1]

4. The inheritance of the Levites was a shadow of the New Testament believer's life. Look up Deuteronomy 10:8-9 and explain in your own words how these verses describe your spiritual birthright.

Tuesday

1. Read and meditate on Psalm 42 (supplemental reading: II Corinthians 1).

2. Write out Psalm 84:5.

3. In Psalm 84:5-7, the author describes the happy procession of pilgrims who are thronging together on their way to one of the great Feasts in Zion, the city of the King. Although they must pass through the "Valley of Baca" (Valley of Weeping), the Lord makes it a place of blessing. This passage provides an apt picture of the Christian journey as well. With this in mind, rewrite the six phrases found in these verses in your own words

Psalm 84:5a

Psalm 84:5b

Psalm 84:6a

Psalm 84:6b

Psalm 84:7a

Psalm 84:7b

Tuesday - *continued*

4. Psalm 42 could very well be a commentary on Psalm 84:6. Review Psalm 42 and explain in your own words what it is like to go through deep sorrow or adversity knowing that you can call out to the Lord in the midst of it.

5. Look up Ephesians 2:1-3, 12. Do you remember what life was like when you were separated from God? Paul once said that in the midst of the great adversity he continually faced, he was "perplexed, but not despairing." (II Corinthians 4:8) Explain the difference between being discouraged or "perplexed" as a believer and the despair that comes to those who don't know Christ.

Wednesday

1. Read and meditate on Psalm 84 (supplemental reading: II Corinthians 6).

2. Write out Psalm 84:10.

3. Read the following commentary on Psalm 84:10 by Albert Barnes and describe what you learn.

> When we come to the end of life - to the time when we shall review the past, and ask where we have found most true happiness, most that was satisfactory to the soul, most that we shall delight then to dwell on and to remember, most that we should be glad to have repeated and perpetuated, most that would be free from the remembrance of disappointment, chagrin, and care - it will not be the banqueting hall - the scenes of gaiety - the honors, the praises, the flatteries of people - or even the delights of literature and of the social circle - but it will be the happy times which we shall have spent in communion with God...[2]

4. One of the clearest examples of what Mr. Barnes writes above is the life of Moses. Read Hebrews 11:24-27. Imagine him sitting on top of Mount Nebo at the end of his life, reflecting upon the enormous decision he made 80 years earlier. Describe what he might have thought about the other path his life could have taken had he chosen it. What did he lose and what did he gain by the choice he made? Explain your answers.

Wednesday - continued

5. Read Psalm 84:1-7 in *The New Living Translation* (NLT) and write out what fresh insights or perspectives you gain.

> How lovely is your dwelling place, O Lord of Heaven's Armies. I long, yes, I faint with longing to enter the courts of the Lord. With my whole being, body and soul, I will shout joyfully to the living God. Even the sparrow finds a home, and the swallow builds her nest and raises her young at a place near your altar, O Lord of Heaven's Armies, my King and my God! What joy for those who can live in your house, always singing your praises. *Interlude*
>
> What joy for those whose strength comes from the Lord, who have set their minds on a pilgrimage to Jerusalem. When they walk through the Valley of Weeping, it will become a place of refreshing springs. The autumn rains will clothe it with blessings. They will continue to grow stronger, and each of them will appear before God in Jerusalem.

Thursday

1. Read and meditate on Psalm 27:1-6 (supplemental reading: II Samuel 7).

2. Write out Psalm 27:4.

3. Look up the word *dwell* (Heb. *yashab*3427) in a Bible dictionary and describe what you learn.

4. Look up the following verses and explain what you learn about this Hebraic word.

    Psalm 23:6

    Psalm 68:6

    Psalm 84:4

    Psalm 91:1

    Psalm 101:6-7

    Psalm 140:13

    Isaiah 6:1

5. Read through the following translations (and paraphrases) of Psalm 27:4 and explain what you learn about David's perspective of the house of the Lord.

    "The one thing I want from God, the thing I seek most of all, is the privilege of meditating in his Temple, living in his presence every day of my life, delighting in his incomparable perfections and glory." (Liv)

    "One prayer have I made to the Lord, and this is my heart's desire; that I may have a place in the house of the Lord all the days of my life, looking on his glory, and getting wisdom in his Temple." (BBE)

    "One thing have I asked of the Lord, that will I seek, inquire for, and (insistently) require: that I may dwell in the house of the Lord (in His presence) all the days of my life, to behold and gaze upon the beauty (the sweet attractiveness and the delightful loveliness) of the Lord and to meditate, consider, and inquire in His temple." (AMP)

Friday

1. Read and meditate on Psalm 27:1-6 (supplemental reading: Joshua 7).

2. Write out Psalm 27:5.

3. Look up the word which is translated as *secret place* (Heb. *cether*5643) in a Bible dictionary and describe what you learn.

4. In biblical times, when many people lived in tents, they would typically bury their valuables in the dirt, somewhere within their tents. One negative example of this is found in Joshua 7:21. Look up this passage and then use it to illustrate how the Lord protects His people.

5. Look up the following verses and explain what you learn about this Hebraic word.

    I Samuel 19:2

    Job 22:14

    Psalm 18:11

    Psalm 31:20

    Psalm 32:7

    Psalm 61:4

    Psalm 91:1

    Psalm 119:114

Saturday

1. Read and meditate on Psalm 65 (supplemental reading: I John 3).

2. Write out Psalm 65:4.

3. For the most part, the Old Testament saint focused on the outward aspects of religion. But Isaiah 57:15 offers one of those rare glimpses of one's inward life with God. Read Isaiah 57:15 and explain in your own words what you learn.

4. In the New Testament, the inward life of the believer is emphasized. The term *abide* (Gk. *men* 3306) corresponds with the Hebrew term *yashab* and was a favorite term of the apostle John. Look up the following passages from his writings and describe what you learn from each of them.

   John 15:4-6

   John 15:9-10

   I John 2:28

   I John 3:6, 9

Saturday - *continued*

I John 3:14-17

5. Write out three of John's statements from the verses above, replacing the word *abides in* with *lives in and makes his home in*.

   a.

   b.

   c.

Sunday

1. Read and meditate on Psalm 84 (supplemental reading: I John 4).

2. Review your answer to question 4 in Monday's homework and explain how you are appropriating all that comes with your "spiritual birthright."

3. Review your answer to question 5 in Tuesday's homework and read II Corinthians 1:3-5. Describe a period of your life where you felt greatly discouraged and yet, at the same time, sensed the Holy Spirit comforting you through it.

4. Review question 4 in yesterday's homework and read John 15 and I John 3 in their entirety. Can you see how closely aligned the subjects of *abiding* and *love* are to each other? The key to this spiritual connection is found in I John 4:16. Write out this verse in your own words and do your best to explain it. Also, describe how you sense God's love for other people indwelling you and reaching out to them.

WEEK 9: THE GOODNESS OF GOD

Monday

1. Read and meditate on Psalm 34:8-14 (supplemental reading: Luke 15).

2. Write out Psalm 34:8.

3. Look up the word *good* (Heb. *towb*$_{2896}$) in a Bible dictionary and describe what you learn.

4. To taste something means to try it out for the purpose of determining whether or not one would wish to experience more of it. And such is the case with God's goodness. It simply cannot be understood academically. We do need to read what Scripture says about it, but more importantly is that it becomes real to us. This occurs either through a revelation of the Holy Spirit or through personal experience. This week's Bible studies will emphasize the writings of godly men in the hope that the Holy Spirit will make real to you what God has made known to them. Read the following comments by A.W. Tozer and explain what you learn about the importance of holding a worthy view of the Lord. How was Abraham Lincoln's life a picture of God's benevolent nature?

> History shows that no tribe or nation has ever risen morally above its religion. If it had a debased religion it had a debased people…
>
> Christianity at any given time is strong or weak depending upon her concept of God. And I insist upon this and I have said it many times, that the basic trouble with the Church today is her unworthy conception of God…
> Our religion is little because our god is little. Our religion is weak because our god is weak. Our religion is ignoble because the god we serve is ignoble. We do not see God as He is…
>
> I suppose one of the kindest men in America was Lincoln… [One day an aide said to him,] "Mr. President, you seem very serious today."
>
> "Yes," he said, "today is 'butcher day.' They're going to shoot a lot of boys today in the army for retreating under fire or doing something else in wartime. I don't blame those boys; they weren't cowards. Their legs did it." Along with his tears he said, "I'm going over the list, and I'm going to save every one that I can."
>
> That's why we love Lincoln, not just because he freed the slaves or saved the Union, but because he had a big heart.[1]

Tuesday

1. Read and meditate on Psalm 14 (supplemental reading: Romans 2).

2. Write out Psalm 14:3.

3. Read the following comments by Thomas Chalmers regarding "the riches of God's goodness" and describe what you learn.

    Goodness which remains unequalled and unexhausted after it has been sinned against — the goodness which persists in multiplying upon the transgressor the chances of his recovery, and that in the midst of affront and opposition — the goodness which, loathe to inflict the retaliating blow, still holds out a little longer and a little longer; and, with all the means in its power of avenging the insults of disobedience, still ekes out the season for its return, and plies it with all the encouragements of a free pardon and an offered reconciliation. This is the exuberance of goodness, this is the richness of forbearance and long suffering; and it is the very display which God is now making in reference to our world.

    O my great and good God, who art good in all Thy greatness, and whose chiefest greatness is to be good, how can I possibly think amiss of Thee, distrust Thee, or harbor any jealous apprehensions concerning Thee? And how unworthy should I be of this Thy goodness if I should![2]

4. God's goodness and His kindness are nearly synonymous terms. But there is a deeper truth involved when considering the Lord's attributes: they are infinite, whereas our qualities are very limited. Read the following passage from my book *Living in Victory* and describe what you learn.

    When I think of kindness, a former co-worker named Wilda comes to mind. She was one of the nicest people I have ever known. Since she was also a Jehovah's Witness, I think it safe to assume that her kindness was not of the Lord. She simply had a pleasant and kind disposition.

    When we think of biblical terms such as love, patience, and kindness, we tend to fit those terms into definitions that coincide with our own experiences. When we try to define characteristics of Almighty God in terms we can only relate to with imperfect humans, our definitions tend to be shallow and empty.

    Is God kind like Wilda was kind? Certainly, just like He is powerful like Mike Tyson is powerful. Our kindness is shallow compared to God's burning love for people.[3]

Wednesday

1. Read and meditate on Psalm 31 (supplemental reading: Deuteronomy 8).

2. Write out Psalm 31:19.

3. Read the following commentaries about this verse and describe what you learn about the way God gives out His goodness to those who love Him.

   a. The Divine goodness is not emptied out in heaps at our feet, when we first start in faith's pathway. Rather, it is kept in reserve for us until we need it, and then disbursed...

   The storehouses of goodness are not opened until we come to where they are. They are placed, so to speak, at different points along our path; the right supply always at the right place. At every river there is a bridge. In every desert there are oases, with their springs of water and their palm trees. For those who fear God and walk in His ways there is not a real need of any kind along the entire path to heaven's gate, without its goodness laid up in reserve. But we shall not get the goodness until we reach the point of need, where the supply is laid up.[4]

   b. God does not put His best gifts, so to speak, in the shop-windows; He keeps these in the inner chambers. He does not arrange His gifts as dishonest traders do their wares, putting the finest outside or on the top, and the less good beneath. "Thou hast kept the good wine until now." It is they who inhabit "the secret place of the Most High," and whose lives are filled with communion with Him, realising His presence, seeking to know His will, reaching out the tendrils of their hearts to twine round Him, and diligently, for His dear sake, doing the tasks of life; who taste the selected dainties from God's gracious hands.

   How foolish, then, to [think] that the best good is the good that we can touch and taste and handle and that men can see! No! No! Deep down in our hearts a joy that strangers never intermeddle with nor know, a peace that passes understanding, a present Christ and a Heaven all but present, because Christ is present — these are the good things for men, and these are the things which God does not, because He cannot, fling broadcast into the world, but which He keeps, because He must, for those that desire them, and are fit for them.[5]

Thursday

1. Read and meditate on Psalm 119:65-72 (supplemental reading: Job 1-2).

2. Write out Psalm 119:67 in your own words.

3. One of the great challenges the Lord faces with His children has to do with His desire to do good to them. Too much discipline can crush a man's spirit. Likewise, excessive outward blessings can lead a person away from God and into carnality. The Lord must continually balance all of His dealings with His children. Read Deuteronomy 8:7-14 and explain what you think the Lord was concerned about. Then describe the challenge He faces with blessing American Christians.

4. Read Job 1:6-11 and describe Satan's accusation. If the devil were to make the same accusation about you to God, how accurate would it be? Explain your answer.

5. Compare Psalm 145:9 with Matthew 5:45. Then read the following commentary on Psalm 145:9 by Charles Spurgeon and explain what you learn—especially in light of Matthew 5:45.

> Kindness is a law of God's universe, the world was planned for happiness; even now that sin has so sadly marred God's handiwork, and introduced elements which were not from the beginning, the Lord has so arranged matters that the fall is broken, the curse is met by an antidote, and the inevitable pain is softened with mitigations. Even in this sin-stricken world, under its disordered economy, there are abundant traces of a hand skilful to soothe distress and heal disease. That which makes life bearable is the tenderness of the great Father.[6]

Friday

1. Read and meditate on Psalm 143 (supplemental reading: Genesis 24).

2. Write out Psalm 143:10, but replace the word *good* with at least three different synonyms (e.g., bountiful, etc.).

3. Read through the following Bible translations of the three verses that are provided below and explain any ways that God's goodness becomes more real to you. Compare each verse with the translation you normally use.

   Psalm 31:19

   "How wonderful are the good things you keep for those who honor you! Everyone knows how good you are, how securely you protect those who trust you." (GNB)

   "How great is the goodness you have stored up for those who fear you. You lavish it on those who come to you for protection, blessing them before the watching world." (NLT)

   "Oh, how great is your goodness to those who publicly declare that you will rescue them. For you have stored up great blessings for those who trust and reverence you." (Liv)

   Psalm 34:10

   "The renegade may be in need, and go hungry; but those who search for the Lord shall not be short of anything good." (Har)

   "Apostates may be famishing and starving, but those who turn to the Eternal lack no good." (Mof)

   "Even strong young lions sometimes go hungry, but those who trust in the Lord will lack no good thing." (NLT)

   Psalm 145:9

   "He is good to everyone, and his compassion is intertwined with everything he does." (Liv)

   "The Lord is universally kind; Yahweh's tenderness embraces all his creatures." (Jer)

   "The Eternal is good to all who look to him, and his compassion covers all that he has made." (Mof)

Saturday

1. Read and meditate on Psalm 125 (supplemental reading: Revelation 22).

2. Write out Psalm 125:4-5 in your own words.

3. One of the unavoidable laws of God's kingdom is that of sowing and reaping. It could be rightly said that we determine our own Judgment Day by the way we live our lives. Look up the following verses in Proverbs 11 and explain what you learn about this spiritual law.

    Proverbs 11:5

    Proverbs 11:17

    Proverbs 11:23-31

4. Look up Romans 2:4 and then read the following commentary by Martyn Lloyd-Jones regarding those who skew God's character by emphasizing His goodness to the exclusion of His wrath. Have you ever been guilty of what he is describing? Have you witnessed teachers do what he is referring to? Explain how Mr. Lloyd-Jones' comments help to balance your perspectives about the Lord.

    This attitude of despising God's goodness and longsuffering is guilty also in that it obviously regards God's goodness as something which, as it were, gives us license to sin and to go on sinning. In other words, it regards God's love and mercy and compassion and forbearance as being something weak and flabby...

Saturday - continued

So to hold this view of God's goodness is tantamount to despising the very character of God, it is to say that God Himself is indulgent towards sin… There is surely nothing more insulting to God than just that very attitude, and what it leads to is that God's justice and righteousness are put on an even lower plane than the law of the land…

These people are primarily concerned about going on with the sinful kind of life which appeals to them. So they are unconsciously constructing a god for themselves who will allow them to do that. They are using God's goodness as a license and a liberty, a cloak and an excuse for their own sin… They are manipulating, or trying to manipulate, even the character of God to serve their own ends. Man is the center. What a man wants to do, what man likes doing, must be supreme; and God has got to be modified to fit in with what I want to do, and what I like. In other words, modern theology, liberalism, is thoroughly subjective. It starts with a man, and everything has to be accommodated to suit man.[7]

1. Read and meditate on Psalm 45 (supplemental reading: II Peter 3).

2. Write out Psalm 45:1.

3. Read the following comments about God's goodness from the *Pulpit Commentary*.[8] For each point listed, describe in detail how the statement has been true in your life.

   a. "The goodness of God ought to be one of the strongest barriers that can be raised up against sin."

   b. "The goodness of God should 'lead us to repentance.'"

   c. "The goodness of God should lead us to do good to others."

   d. "The goodness of God to us in this world should inspire us with confidence in his goodness to us in the world to come."

WEEK 10: THOSE WHO FEAR HIM

 Monday

1. Read and meditate on Psalm 90 (supplemental reading: Genesis 20).

2. Write out Psalm 90:11-12.

3. Read through the following verses that are provided below in the *King James Version* and the *Amplified Bible* and explain what you learn about the fearfulness of God from each verse.

    Psalm 47:2

    > "For the LORD most high is terrible; he is a great King over all the earth." (KJV)

    > "For the Lord Most High excites terror, awe, and dread; He is a great King over all the earth." (AMP)

    Psalm 66:3

    > "Say unto God, How terrible art thou in thy works! through the greatness of thy power shall thine enemies submit themselves unto thee." (KJV)

    > "Say to God, How awesome and fearfully glorious are Your works! Through the greatness of Your power shall Your enemies submit themselves to You [*with feigned and reluctant obedience*]." (AMP)

    Psalm 66:5

    > "Come and see the works of God: he is terrible in his doing toward the children of men." (KJV)

    > "Come and see the works of God; see how [*to save His people He smites their foes; He is*] terrible in His doings toward the children of men." (AMP)

Monday - continued

Psalm 68:35

"O God, thou art terrible out of thy holy places: the God of Israel is he that giveth strength and power unto his people. Blessed be God." (KJV)

"O God, awe-inspiring, profoundly impressive, and terrible are You out of Your holy places; the God of Israel Himself gives strength and fullness of might to His people. Blessed be God!" (AMP)

4. Read the following comments by Mike Yaconelli and describe what you learn.

The tragedy of modern faith is that we no longer are capable of being terrified... I would like to suggest that the Church become a place of terror again; a place where God continually has to tell us, "Fear not;" a place where our relationship with God is not a simple belief or a doctrine or theology, it is God's burning presence in our lives. I am suggesting that the tame God of relevance be replaced by the God whose very presence shatters our egos into dust, burns our sin into ashes, and strips us naked to reveal the real person within. The Church needs to become a gloriously dangerous place where nothing is safe in God's presence except us. Nothing—including our plans, our agendas, our priorities, our politics, our money, our security, our comfort, our possessions, our needs.[1]

Tuesday

1. Read and meditate on Psalm 99 (supplemental reading: Exodus 19).

2. Write out Psalm 99:3.

3. Read the following two stories and explain what you learn about the fearful side of God.

    Leviticus 10:1-3

    Acts 5:1-11

4. Look up the following verses and explain what you learn about the fearfulness of God.

    II Chronicles 19:7

    Psalm 119:120

    Isaiah 66:2

    Luke 12:5

    Romans 11:20-22

Tuesday - continued

II Corinthians 5:9-11

II Corinthians 6:16-7:1

Philippians 2:12

Hebrews 10:26-29

Hebrews 12:28-29

I Peter 1:17-19

Wednesday

1. Read and meditate on Psalm 33 (supplemental reading: Proverbs 2).

2. Write out Psalm 33:18.

3. Look up the word *fear* (Heb. *yare'*$_{3372}$) in a Bible dictionary and describe what you learn.

4. Write out, in your own words, each of the following verses about the benefits of fearing the Lord.

   Psalm 85:9

   Psalm 111:5

   Psalm 115:13

   Psalm 145:19

   Psalm 147:11

Wednesday - *continued*

Proverbs 9:10

Proverbs 10:27

Proverbs 14:27

Proverbs 19:23

Proverbs 22:4

Isaiah 33:6

Thursday

1. Read and meditate on Psalm 103 (supplemental reading: Acts 5).

2. Write out Psalm 103:11.

3. Carefully read the following quotes about the fear of the Lord and explain in your own words what you learn from each one.

   a. "Fear, without joy, is torment; and joy, without holy fear, would be presumption." — Charles Spurgeon[2]

   b. "No one can know the true grace of God who has not first known the fear of God... The effort of liberal and borderline modernists to woo men to God by presenting the soft side of religion is an unqualified evil because it ignores the very reason for our alienation from God in the first place." — A.W. Tozer[3]

   c. "Men are more apt to presume than to despair, and if despair hath killed her thousands, presumption hath killed her ten thousands." — A. Farindon[4]

   d. "The opposite of the fear of the Lord is presumption and entitlement: 'You owe it to me, God!' That is an attitude that underlies much of modern Christianity." — Steve Gallagher

   e. "In a Christian's course fear and love must go together. In heaven, love will absorb fear. No one now can love God aright without fearing Him. Self-confident men, who do not know their own hearts, or the reasons they have for being dissatisfied with themselves, do not fear God, and they think this bold freedom is to love Him. We cannot understand Christ's mercies till we understand His power, His glory, His unspeakable holiness, and our demerits; that is, until we first fear Him." — J. H. Newman[5]

Friday

1. Read and meditate on Psalm 103 (supplemental reading: Revelation 6).

2. Write out Psalm 103:17.

3. We've studied quite a few Scriptures about the fear of the Lord, but it's almost as if we have skirted the edges of what it actually is. Rewrite Proverbs 9:10 in your own words; do your best to "get out of the box" with your wording.

4. My friend David Ravenhill says, "Fear means fear! If you were to stand on the edge of the roof of a five-story building, a very strong sense of apprehension would overtake you. That is the sense we should have of this holy God Whom we have repeatedly offended by our sin."

   Solomon says that it is precisely this feeling of trepidation that opens the door to wisdom about God's kingdom. The word "wisdom" in the Old Testament is comparable to the New Testament concept of salvation. Accompanying any true conversion is a very real sense of the spiritual danger the person is in. It is that fear of the consequences of his rebellion that drives him into contrition and repentance. Review Psalm 103:10-12 and explain the benefits that come as a result of conversion.

Friday - continued

5. There is also a wrong type of fear of God. It comes about when a person is aware of the consequences of sin and self-will but are unwilling to repent. Allow me to share a couple of examples of this. Explain in your own words what you learn from each of these stories.

In Matthew 25 we find the parable of the "Talents." Two of the servants were rewarded for their efforts on behalf of their master. Please read the account of the third servant in Matthew 25:24-30 before proceeding.

This man had been told to accomplish his master's wishes while he was away. His excuse was that he became paralyzed by fear of his master. Of course, if he really did fear his master he would have been all the more diligent to please him. His response reveals his actual attitude; *viz.*, no matter what he would ever do, nothing would satisfy his boss. To avoid doing what he really didn't want to do in the first place, he simply maligned his master's character to justify his laziness.

The second example is found in Revelation 6:12-17. This passage describes the breaking of the Sixth Seal—the unveiling of Jesus Christ to the world. Those who love Him will not be terror-stricken when He returns. However, the response will be completely different with those who are living in self-will.

Perhaps these two responses could be understood more clearly with an illustration. Imagine a group of teenagers in a park, minding their own business, when a gang of armed thugs comes up and begins to intimidate them. All of the sudden, several police cruisers swoop into the park and surround the group. The innocent teens feel a great sense of relief, while the gangbangers become full of consternation. This is a picture of what it will be like when the Lord returns to earth.

1. Read and meditate on Psalm 103 (supplemental reading: Luke 19).

2. Write out Psalm 103:13.

3. Read the following commentary by Charles Spurgeon and describe what you learn.

As a father takes pleasure in his own children, so doth the Lord solace himself in his own beloved ones, whose marks of new birth are fear and hope. They fear, for they are sinners; they hope, for God is merciful. They fear him, for he is great; they hope in him, for he is good. Their fear sobers their hope; their hope brightens their fear: God takes pleasure in them both in their trembling and in their rejoicing.[6]

3. Read the following passages of Scripture from *The Amplified Bible* and explain what you learn and how it affects you.

Psalm 103:11-13

"For as the heavens are high above the earth, so great are His mercy and loving-kindness toward those who reverently and worshipfully fear Him. As far as the east is from the west, so far has He removed our transgressions from us. As a father loves and pities his children, so the Lord loves and pities those who fear Him [*with reverence, worship, and awe*]."

Psalm 103:17-18

"But the mercy and loving-kindness of the Lord are from everlasting to everlasting upon those who reverently and worshipfully fear Him, and His righteousness is to children's children. To such as keep His covenant [*hearing, receiving, loving, and obeying it*] and to those who [*earnestly*] remember His commandments to do them [*imprinting them on their hearts*]."

Sunday

1. Read and meditate on Psalm 86 (supplemental reading: Revelation 3).

2. Write out Psalm 86:11 and then explain in your own words what you think it means.

3. Review the verses in question 3 of Monday's homework. Do you feel that you have had a proper comprehension of God's fearful nature? Explain your answer.

4. Review the comments by Mike Yaconelli in question 4 of Monday's homework. Do his statements describe attitudes that you have held about God? Explain your answer.

5. Choose three of the comments in question 3 of Thursday's homework and explain how they are or are not descriptive of your Christian life. Explain your answers.

   a.

   b.

   c.

WEEK 11: GOD REIGNS

Monday

1. Read and meditate on Psalm 11 and 12 (supplemental reading: I Samuel 8).

2. Write out Psalm 11:4.

3. Psalms 11 and 12 tell of a time when society on the whole had turned bad. The friend of David who moaned, "If the foundations are destroyed, what can the righteous do?" (Psalm 11:3), rightly discerned the age in which he lived. A heavy blanket of evil seemed to rest upon the land. "The god of lies [had become] enthroned in the national heart."[1] There was an acute shortage of godly men. Society seemed to have reached the last stage of corruption "when vileness is exalted" and "the wicked strut about on every side." (Psalm 12:8)

   We too live in a day when evil is reaching its climax. Many believers respond to this spiritual blight with the same defeatist attitude expressed by David's timid friend. "No matter how hard we try to live godly lives, the world around us only gets darker. It's hopeless to fight this losing battle! What can a righteous man do but bend to such times?"

   The comfort to the believer comes from the assurance that Jehovah is still on His throne. He still controls the affairs of mankind. Psalm 11:4 is a great encouragement for those of us who are determined to live godly lives in the midst of a wicked generation.

   Choose four verses from Psalm 11 and 12 that you feel are applicable to our own culture. Rewrite them in your own words regarding what you see around you.

   a.

   b.

Monday - *continued*

    c.

    d.

4. Consider what David's friend surmised in Psalm 11:1-3. What would you say to a friend who made a statement like this regarding the United States?

Tuesday

1. Read and meditate on Psalm 93 (supplemental reading: Revelation 4).

2. Rewrite Psalm 93:1-2 in your own words.

3. Look up the word *reigns* (Heb. *malak*4427) in a Bible dictionary and describe what you learn.

4. Read the following passages of Scripture and explain what you Lord about God's sovereign rule over the earth.

   Psalm 47:2-3

   Psalm 96:3-10

   Psalm 97:1-9

   Psalm 103:19-21

   Psalm 146:6-10

Wednesday

1. Read and meditate on Psalm 99 (supplemental reading: Proverbs 8).

2. Write out Psalm 99:1.

3. Read Psalm 33:6-11 in the translations provided and write out what fresh insights or perspectives you gain.

   Psalm 33:6 "At the bidding of the Lord the heavens were formed, and all their company at his decree." (Har)

   Psalm 33:7 "He assigned the sea its boundaries and locked the oceans in vast reservoirs." (NLT)

   Psalm 33:8 "Let everyone in all the world—men, women and children—fear the Lord and stand in awe of him." (Liv)

   Psalm 33:9 "For He spoke, and it came into being; He commanded, and it came into existence." (Hol)

   Psalm 33:10 "The Eternal wrecks the purposes of pagans, he brings to nothing what the nations plan." (Mof)

   Psalm 33:11 "But the Lord's plans stand firm forever; his intentions can never be shaken." (NLT)

Wednesday - continued

4. Read Psalm 99:1-5 in the translations provided and write out what fresh insights or perspectives you gain.

   Psalm 99:1 "The Lord is sovereign; let pagan nations tremble. He is enthroned in heaven; let the earth quake." (Har)

   Psalm 99:2 "Great is the Lord who dwells in Zion, sovereign ruler of all peoples!" (Knox)

   Psalm 99:3 "Let them praise thy great and terrible name; for it is holy." (KJV)

   Psalm 99:4 "You are a king who loves justice, insisting on honesty, justice, virtue, as you have done for Jacob." (Jer)

   Psalm 99:5 "Give high honour to the Lord our God, worshipping at his feet; holy is he." (BBE)

Thursday

1. Read and meditate on Psalm 139 (supplemental reading: Jonah 1-4).

2. Write out Psalm 139:5.

3. Read Job 23:13-14 and explain what you learn about God's dealings with His sons.

4. Read the book of Jonah, paying careful attention to God's sovereign actions in the prophet's life. Look at the following verses and explain in your own words what you learn about God's efforts to compel Jonah to do His will or to teach him a valuable lesson.

   Jonah 1:4

   Jonah 1:15

   Jonah 1:17

   Jonah 2:10

   Jonah 3:1

   Jonah 4:6

   Jonah 4:7

   Jonah 4:8

Friday

1. Read and meditate on Psalm 139 (supplemental reading: Hebrews 12).

2. Write out Psalm 139:17-18 in your own words.

3. Read the following passage from my book *Living in Victory* and describe what you learn about God's sovereignty in your life.

> The fact of the matter is that God has been deeply involved with your life since your birth. You have been the focus of an immense heavenly operation for many years. Who can know the number of angels assigned at various times to watch over you? Who can guess how many people God has used in a myriad of ways to influence and mold your life, to bring you to the point of seeing your great need for Him? How many different circumstances of your life—loss, failures, problems, difficult people — did God use to bring you to that momentous decision? Paul rightly said, "You were bought with a price…" Of course the greatest price paid was on Calvary, but how much else has gone into our salvation?
>
> Unquestionably, God has been intricately involved in the life of every single person who comes to Him…
>
> One of my wife's most endearing characteristics is her insistence upon being involved with me constantly. For instance, when I wake up in the middle of the night (I am a chronic insomniac), her eyes immediately pop open to see what I'm doing. If I get out of bed to read or do something to avoid bothering her, she insists on me staying there, even though turning the light on means she will lose sleep. My wife wants to be involved with everything that goes on with me. It isn't out of nosiness or out of being insecure. She simply loves me and is absorbed in every phase of my life. To Kathy, love equates with undying interest.
>
> So it is with God. He has a tremendous investment in every believer's life and is greatly interested in every aspect of it.[2]

Saturday

1. Read and meditate on Psalm 139 (supplemental reading: I Peter 1).

2. Write out Psalm 139:8.

3. Read the following commentary by Charles Spurgeon and describe what you learn.

> *"If I ascend up into heaven, thou art there."* Filling the loftiest region with his yet loftier presence, Jehovah is in the heavenly place, at home, upon his throne. The ascent, if it were possible, would be unavailing for purposes of escape; it would, in fact, be a flying into the centre of the fire to avoid the heat. There would he be immediately confronted by the terrible personality of God. Note the abrupt words - "Thou, there."
>
> *"If I make my bed in hell, behold, thou art there."* Descending into the lowest imaginable depths among the dead, there should we find the Lord. Thou! says the Psalmist, as if he felt that God was the one great Existence in all places... A *"behold"* is added to the second clause, since it seems more a wonder to meet with God in hell than in heaven, in Hades than in Paradise.
>
> Of course the presence of God produces very different effects in these places, but it is unquestionably in each; the bliss of one, the terror of the other. What an awful thought, that some men seem resolved to take up their night's abode in hell, a night which shall know no morning.[3]

4. Read Psalm 139:2-10 in *The NET Bible* (NET) and write out what fresh insights or perspectives you gain.

> You know when I sit down and when I get up; even from far away you understand my motives. You carefully observe me when I travel or when I lie down to rest; you are aware of everything I do. Certainly my tongue does not frame a word without you, O Lord, being thoroughly aware of it. You squeeze me in from behind and in front; you place your hand on me. Your knowledge is beyond my comprehension; it is so far beyond me, I am unable to fathom it. Where can I go to escape your spirit? Where can I flee to escape your presence? If I were to ascend to heaven, you would be there. If I were to sprawl out in Sheol, there you would be. If I were to fly away on the wings of the dawn, and settle down on the other side of the sea, even there your hand would guide me, your right hand would grab hold of me.

Sunday

1. Read and meditate on Psalm 139 (supplemental reading: I Corinthians 13).

2. Write out Psalm 139:23-24.

3. Read Hosea 2:6-7 and explain what you learn about God's dealings with those who go back into a life of pursuing sin.

4. Every true believer has a hedge around his life that keeps him within certain boundaries of behavior. When he begins to stray off the narrow way, the Holy Spirit is there to impede his progress. But people differ in how they respond to this divine constraint. The *Pulpit Commentary* exposes the difference between the person who sees God's will as a bother and the one who sees it as a blessing. Read the following passage and explain in your own words what you learn. Which of these descriptions are most applicable to your life? Explain your answer.

   Divine limitations are felt to be irksome to us when our will is in conflict with God's will... But we men on earth live in frequent conflict with our heavenly Father's will. We find the walls to be hard because we fling ourselves upon them. Our chain galls us because we chafe and fret ourselves against it. The wandering sheep is torn by the hedge, while the quiet obedient sheep knows nothing of the briars. When we rebel against God we murmur at his restraints...

   Far the highest obedience is not the restraint of our will before God's will, but the assimilation of the two. We learn to will what God wills. Then we keep within the Divine limitations, and yet they cease to be limitations to us. They never touch us because we never attempt nor wish to cross them. Here lies the secret of peace as well as of holiness. So lofty an attainment can only be reached through that oneness with Christ of which he speaks when he prays that his disciples may be one with him and the Father, as he is one with the Father (John 17:21).[4]

WEEK 12: OH, PRAISE HIM!

Monday

1. Read and meditate on Psalm 30 (supplemental reading: II Samuel 6).

2. Write out Psalm 30:4.

3. In Psalm 30:5, we are given two reasons why should "sing praise" and "give thanks" to the Lord. Rewrite these two phrases in your own words, keeping in mind the way He has dealt with you in the past.

    Psalm 30:5a

    Psalm 30:5b

4. In Psalm 30:6, David recalls a time in his life when prosperity had caused him to lose his dependence upon God. One would expect prosperity to make believers more grateful to the Lord but actually just the opposite is the case. The more comfort, security and pleasure we enjoy, the less we think about God; hence, the less gratitude we feel towards Him. Read the following commentary by Albert Barnes and describe what you learn.

    They become worldly-minded, and it is necessary for God to teach them how easily he can sweep all this away - and thus to bring them back to a right view of the uncertainty of all earthly things. Health fails, or friends die, or property takes wings and flies away; and God accomplishes his purpose - a purpose invaluable to them - by showing them their dependence on Himself, and by teaching them that permanent and certain happiness and security are to be found in Him alone.[1]

5. There are different opinions as to what occasioned the writing of this psalm. Some scholars believe that it was written at the dedication of the tabernacle. Others believe David wrote it when his palace was completed on Mt. Zion. Still others think that it was composed for the dedication of the Temple. Whatever the case may be, Psalm 30:11 is very reminiscent of the story found in II Samuel 6:12-19. Read this story and describe any comparisons you see with Psalm 30:11.

1. Read and meditate on Psalm 100 (supplemental reading: John 10).

2. Write out Psalm 100:3.

3. Some people might feel as though Psalm 100:3 is out of place in a psalm full of adoration of Jehovah. But actually this verse expresses a vital aspect of praise that is typically overlooked by most Christians.

   In both Hebrew and Greek, the term *worship* conveys the idea of physically prostrating oneself before another. True praise has much more to do with understanding one's proper place before God than it does simply singing lively songs in church. Spend a few minutes pondering the meaning of Psalm 100:3. Can you see how this verse "puts us in our place?" Explain your answer.

4. In Psalm 100 the psalmist calls upon others to express their adoration of the Lord. The first four verses are full of action verbs. List the call to action in each of the following phrases along with an explanation as to what it really means to your life.

   Psalm 100:1

   Psalm 100:2a

   Psalm 100:2b

   Psalm 100:3a

   Psalm 100:4a

   Psalm 100:4b

   Psalm 100:4c

Wednesday

1. Read and meditate on Psalm 135 (supplemental reading: Ezekiel 20).

2. Write out Psalm 135:5.

3. Read the following comment from the *Pulpit Commentary* about Psalm 135 and describe what you learn.

   God is worthy of our utmost reverence. "The Lord is good." The truth is too familiar to us to strike us; but if we contrast the character of the God whom we worship with that of the deities of heathen lands (see vers. 15-18), we see and feel how great is our privilege, how excellent a thing it is to pay reverent homage to One who is absolutely pure and true and kind — who is "good" in every attribute, whom we can worship, not only without loss of self-respect, but to our highest spiritual advantage.[2]

4. Read Psalm 135 and count how many times the words "praise" and "bless" are used in regard to the Lord.

   a. Praise:

   b. Bless:

5. Review Psalm 135 and list five things mentioned in this psalm about the Lord that you can honestly praise Him about.

   a.

   b.

   c.

   d.

   e.

Thursday

1. Read and meditate on Psalm 145 (supplemental reading: Psalm 85).

2. Write out Psalm 145:7.

3. Look up the word translated as *eagerly utter* (Heb. *naba'*$_{5042}$) in a Bible dictionary and describe what you learn.

4. Look up the word translated as *shout joyfully* (Heb. *ranan*$_{7442}$) in a Bible dictionary and describe what you learn.

5. Write out in Psalm 145:7 in your own words, employing some of the synonyms of these two terms that you just discovered.

6. Review Psalm 145. Did you notice that this psalm is entirely focused on the Lord? Over and over again David recounts the wonderful attributes of God. List twelve things he expresses about the Lord.

   a.

   b.

   c.

Thursday - continued

d.

e.

f.

g.

h.

i.

k.

l.

m.

Thursday - continued

Friday

1. Read and meditate on Psalm 145 (supplemental reading: Nehemiah 9).

2. Write out Psalm 145:18.

3. Read the following verses in the translations provided and write out what fresh insights or perspectives you gain from each about the importance of offering heartfelt worship to God.

   I Kings 8:23 "Therefore, fear the Lord and worship Him in sincerity and truth. Get rid of the gods your ancestors worshiped beyond the Euphrates River and in Egypt, and worship the Lord." (NET)

   Psalm 17:1 "Lord, consider my just cause! Pay attention to my cry for help! Listen to the prayer I sincerely offer!" (NET)

   Psalm 119:7 "I will praise You with a sincere heart when I learn Your righteous judgments." (Hol)

   Psalm 145:18 "The Lord is near all who cry out to him, all who cry out to him sincerely." (NET)

   Hosea 7:14 "They have not prayed to me sincerely, but instead they throw themselves down and wail as the heathen do. When they pray for grain and wine, they gash themselves like pagans. What rebels they are!" (GNB)

   John 4:24 "God is spirit, and those who worship Him must worship in spirit and truth." (NASB)

   Hebrews 10:22 "So let us come near to God with a sincere heart and a sure faith, with hearts that have been purified from a guilty conscience and with bodies washed with clean water." (GNB)

Saturday

1. Read and meditate on Psalm 145 (supplemental reading: II Chronicles 29).

2. Write out Psalm 145:21.

3. Look up the words *praise* (Heb. *t hillah*₈₄₁₆) and *bless* (Heb. *barak*₁₂₈₈) in a Bible dictionary and do your best to understand how these terms differ from each other. Can you see how they are calling on others to do two separate things? Explain your answers.

4. Read Psalm 145:3 in the translations provided and write out what fresh insights or perspectives you gain about the Lord.

   "…His greatness is [*so vast and deep as to be*] unsearchable." (AMP)

   "Great is the Lord, and marvelous worthy to be praised; there is no end of his greatness." (PBV)

   "Great is the Lord and worthy of all praise; his greatness is unfathomable." (NEB)

   "The Lord is great, and merits the highest praise; His grandeur is limitless." (Har)

   "Can anyone measure the magnificence of Yahweh the great, and his inexpressible grandeur?" (Jer)

   "Great is the Lord, and greatly to be praised; his power may never be searched out." (BBE)

   "Great is the Lord! He is most worthy of praise! No one can measure his greatness." (NLT)

Sunday

1. Read and meditate on Psalm 95 (supplemental reading: I Kings 8).

2. Make a list of 7 things the Lord has provided or done for believers in general that you are grateful for.

   a. e.g., The Bible   b.   c.

   d.   e.   f.

   g.

2. Make a list of 10 things the Lord has done for your own spiritual life that you are grateful for.

   a. e.g., Caused me to see my need for Jesus b.

   c.   d.

   e.   f.

   g.   h.

   i.   j.

3. Make a list of 10 things the Lord has done to bless your life while on earth.

   a. e.g., Helped me to maintain good health. b.

   c.   d.

   e.   f.

   g.   h.

   i.   k.

Sunday - continued

4. Rewrite Psalm 95:1-3 in your own words.

5. Acquire a small notebook or journal and begin keeping a Gratitude List. Every day, write down at least one thing that you are grateful for and then spend some time expressing praise to God.

BIBLE TRANSLATIONS

(NLT) *The New Living Translation*, Libronix Digital Library,

(NET) *The NET Bible*, Libronix Digital Library,

(Liv) *The Living Bible*, A.J. Holman Company, 1973, Philadelphia and New York.

(Har) *The Psalms for Today*: A New Translation From the Hebrew Into Current English, by R.K. Harrison. 1961, Zondervan Publishing House.

(NIV) *The New International Version*, Libronix Digital Library,

(Jer) *The Jerusalem Bible*, c 1966 by Darton, Longman, and Todd, Ltd. And Doubleday and Company, Inc.

(AMP) *The Amplified Bible*, e-Sword Bible Program, www.e-sword.net.

(GNB) *The Good News Bible*, e-Sword Bible Program, www.e-sword.net.

(BBE) *1965 Bible in Basic English*, e-Sword Bible Program, www.e-sword.net.

(Ber) *The Modern Language Bible: The New Berkley Version in Modern English*, 1945, 1959, 1969, Zondervan Publishing House.

(ABPS) *The Holy Bible Containing the Old and New Testaments: An Improved Edition*, (American Baptist Publication Society).

(Mof) *A New Translation of the Bible*, by James Moffat, 1954, Harper & Row Publishers.

(KJV) *The King James Version*, e-Sword Bible Program, www.e-sword.net.

(Hol) *The Holman Christian Standard Bible*, Libronix Digital Library,

(Knox) *The Holy Bible: A Translation From the Latin Vulgate in the Light of the Hebrew and Greek Originals*, by Monsignor Ronald Knox, 1954, Sheed & Ward, Inc. and Burns & Oats, Ltd.

(PBV) *The Psalms in the Book of Common Prayer of the Anglican Church*.

(NEB) *The New English Bible*, 1961, Oxford University Press and Cambridge University Press.

NOTES

INTRODUCTION

1. John Ker, as quoted by the *International Standard Bible Encyclopedia, Vol. 8,* as cited in *AGES Digital Library* (Rio, WI: AGES Software, Inc., 2001) p. 897.
2. C.S. Lewis, *The Quotable Lewis* (Wheaton, IL: Tyndale House Publishers, 1989) p. 500.
3. A.R. Faussett, "Introduction to Psalms" *Jamieson, Faussett and Brown Commentary: Old Testament, Vol. 1,* as cited in *AGES Digital Library* (Rio, WI: AGES Software, Inc., 2001) p. 1662.
4. Albert Barnes, "Introduction to Psalms" *Barnes' Notes on the Bible, Vol. 5,* as cited in *AGES Digital Library* (Rio, WI: AGES Software, Inc., 2001) p. 51.

WEEK ONE

1. Albert Barnes, "Psalms: Chapter 1" *Barnes' Notes on the Bible, Vol. 5,* as cited in *AGES Digital Library* (Rio, WI: AGES Software, Inc., 2001) p. 59.
2. Matthew Henry, "Psalms: Chapter 1" *Matthew Henry's Commentary on the Whole Bible, Vol. 4,* as cited in *AGES Digital Library* (Rio, WI: AGES Software, Inc., 2001) p. 562.
3. *Ibid.,* p. 572.

WEEK TWO

1. C. Clemance, "Psalms: Chapter 16" *The Pulpit Commentary,* as cited in *AGES Digital Library* (Rio, WI: AGES Software, Inc., 2001) p. 11.
2. Roy Hession, *We Would See Jesus* (Fort Washington, PA: Christian Literature Crusade, 1958) p. 26.
3. Albert Barnes, "Psalms: Chapter 16" *Barnes' Notes on the Bible, Vol. 5,* as cited in *AGES Digital Library* (Rio, WI: AGES Software, Inc., 2001) p. 275.
4. Matthew Henry, "Psalms: Chapter 16" *Matthew Henry's Commentary on the Whole Bible, Vol. 4,* as cited in *AGES Digital Library* (Rio, WI: AGES Software, Inc., 2001) p. 687.

WEEK THREE

1. Alexander MacLaren, "Psalms: Chapter 23" *Whole Bible Sermon Collection,* as cited in *AGES Digital Library,* (Rio, WI: AGES Software, Inc., 2001) p. 71.
2. John Trapp, "Psalms: Chapter 25" as quoted in C.H. Spurgeon *The Treasury of David, Vol. 1,* (Grand Rapids, MI: Zondervan Publishing House, 1966) p. 411.
3. W. Forsyth, "Psalms: Chapter 25" *The Pulpit Commentary,* as cited in *AGES Digital Library* (Rio, WI: AGES Software, Inc., 2001) p. 20.
4. Albert Barnes, "Psalms: Chapter 25" *Barnes' Notes on the Bible, Vol. 5,* as cited in *AGES Digital Library* (Rio, WI: AGES Software, Inc., 2001) p. 462.
5. Fanny J. Crosby, "All the Way My Savior Leads Me" *The Baptist Hymnal* (Nashville, TN: Convention Press, 1991) p. 62.

WEEK FOUR

1. Charles Caldwell Ryrie, *The Ryrie Study Bible* (Chicago: Moody Press) p. 798.
2. Charles Spurgeon, "Psalms: Chapter 35" as quoted in C.H. Spurgeon *The Treasury of David, Vol. 1* (Grand Rapids, MI: Zondervan Publishing House, 1966) p. 141.
3. Steve Gallagher, *At the Altar of Sexual Idolatry* (Dry Ridge, KY: Pure Life Ministries, 1986, 2000 & 2007) p. 231.

WEEK FIVE

1. Steve Gallagher, *Living in Victory* (Dry Ridge, KY: Pure Life Ministries, 2002) p. 84.
2. *Ibid*, pps. 15-16.
3. *Ibid*, p. 150.

WEEK SIX

1. Rex Andrews, *What the Bible Teaches About Mercy* (Zion, IL: Zion Faith Homes, 1985) p. 15.
2. Charles Spurgeon, "Psalms: Chapter 91" as quoted in C.H. Spurgeon *The Treasury of David, Vol. 2* (Grand Rapids, MI: Zondervan Publishing House, 1966) pps. 88-89.

WEEK SEVEN

1. "Psalms: Chapter 27: The Reward of Diligent Search" *The Pulpit Commentary*, as cited in *AGES Digital Library* (Rio, WI: AGES Software, Inc., 2001) p. 8.
2. A.W. Tozer, *The Pursuit of God* (Camp Hill, PA: Christian Publications, Inc., 1981) pps. 17-18.
3. Steve Gallagher, "Spiritual Refreshment in a Dry and Weary Land" http://www.purelifeministries.org/index.cfm?pageid=163&articleid=127.
4. W. Forsyth, "Psalms: Chapter 63" *The Pulpit Commentary*, as cited in *AGES Digital Library* (Rio, WI: AGES Software, Inc., 2001) p. 7.

WEEK EIGHT

1. Matthew Henry, "Psalms: Chapter 84" *Matthew Henry's Commentary on the Whole Bible, Vol. 4,* as cited in *AGES Digital Library* (Rio, WI: AGES Software, Inc., 2001) p. 1334.
2. Albert Barnes, "Psalms: Chapter 84" *Barnes' Notes on the Bible, Vol. 5,* as cited in *AGES Digital Library* (Rio, WI: AGES Software, Inc., 2001) p. 1385.

WEEK NINE

1. A. W. Tozer, *The Attributes of God, A Journey into the Father's Heart* (Camp Hill, PA: Christian Publications, Inc., 1997) pps. 39, 52.
2. T. Chalmers, D.D., "Romans: Chapter 2" *The Biblical Illustrator,* as cited in *AGES Digital Library* (Rio, WI: AGES Software, Inc., 2001) p. 20.
3. Steve Gallagher, *Living in Victory* (Dry Ridge, KY: Pure Life Ministries, 2002) p. 80.
4. J.R. Miller, D.D., "Psalms: Chapter 31" *The Biblical Illustrator,* as cited in *AGES Digital Library* (Rio, WI: AGES Software, Inc., 2001) p. 44.
5. Alexander MacLaren, "Goodness Wrought and Goodness Laid Up" *Whole Bible Sermon Collection,* as cited in *AGES Digital Library* (Rio, WI: AGES Software, Inc., 2001) p. 134.
6. Charles Spurgeon, "Psalms: Chapter 145" as quoted in C.H. Spurgeon *The Treasury of David, Vol. 3* (Grand Rapids, MI: Zondervan Publishing House, 1966) p. 378.
7. D. Martyn Lloyd-Jones, *Romans, The Righteous Judgment of God* (Edinburgh, Great Britain: The Banner of Truth Trust, 1989) pps. 46-49.
8. R. Tuck, "Psalms: Chapter 100" *The Pulpit Commentary,* as cited in *AGES Digital Library* (Rio, WI: AGES Software, Inc., 2001) p. 16.

WEEK TEN

1. Mike Yaconelli, *The Fear of God*, www.acts17-11.com/fear.html.
2. Charles Spurgeon, "Psalms Chapter 2" as quoted in C.H. Spurgeon *The Treasury of David, Vol. 1* (Grand Rapids, MI: Zondervan Publishing House, 1966) p. 13.

3. A.W. Tozer, quoted from a sermon entitled, *The Terror of the Lord*, http://www.acts17-11.com/snip_tozer_terror.html.
4. A. Farindon, D.D., "Romans: Chapter 11" *Biblical Illustrator,* as cited in *AGES Digital Library* (Rio, WI: AGES Software, Inc., 2001) p. 50.
5. J. H. Newman, B. D., "Psalms: Chapter 2" *Biblical Illustrator,* as cited in *AGES Digital Library* (Rio, WI: AGES Software, Inc., 2001) p. 37.
6. Charles Spurgeon, "Psalms: Chapter 147" as quoted in C.H. Spurgeon *The Treasury of David, Vol. 3* (Grand Rapids, MI: Zondervan Publishing House, 1966) pps. 417-418.

WEEK ELEVEN

1. C. Short, "Psalms: Chapter 12" *The Pulpit Commentary,* as cited in *AGES Digital Library* (Rio, WI: AGES Software, Inc., 2001) p. 10.
2. Steve Gallagher, *Living in Victory* (Dry Ridge, KY: Pure Life Ministries, 2002) pps. 121-122.
3. Charles Spurgeon, "Psalms: Chapter 139" as quoted in C.H. Spurgeon *The Treasury of David, Vol. 3* (Grand Rapids, MI: Zondervan Publishing House, 1966) pps. 260-261.
4. W.F. Adeney, "Lamentations: Chapter 3" *The Pulpit Commentary,* as cited in *AGES Digital Library* (Rio, WI: AGES Software, Inc., 2001) p.

WEEK TWELVE

1. Albert Barnes, "Psalms: Chapter 30" *Barnes' Notes on the Bible , Vol. 5,* as cited in *AGES Digital Library* (Rio, WI: AGES Software, Inc., 2001) p. 525.
2. "Psalms: Chapter 135: Reasons for the Worship and Service of God" *The Pulpit Commentary,* as cited in *AGES Digital Library* (Rio, WI: AGES Software, Inc., 2001) p. 5.

THE WALK OF REPENTANCE

A 24-WEEK GUIDE TO PERSONAL TRANSFORMATION

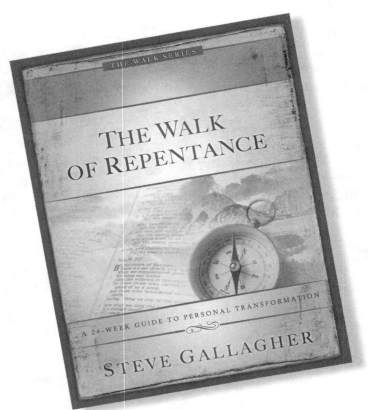

EXPERIENCE THE TIMES OF REFRESHING THAT FOLLOW REPENTANCE

The one thing believers in America don't need more of is information about Christianity. We know more about it than any people who have ever lived. Our problem isn't a lack of knowledge. Our problem is a lack of living it.

This 24-week Bible study has impacted the lives of thousands of people because it equips them to live out the Word of God. It is a simple, straightforward discipleship tool that focuses on the basics of the Christian life. Each week of this easy-to-use curriculum has a theme, addressing the challenges of the Christian life one step at a time.

Whether used by individuals, small groups or couples, in counseling settings, Sunday school classes or prison ministry, *The Walk of Repentance* makes a profound impact and leads sensitive hearts into a deeper intimacy with the Lord.

A Lamp Unto My Feet

A 12-WEEK STUDY THROUGH PSALM 119

EVERY READER WILL BE BROUGHT INTO A DEEPER LOVE, RESPECT AND APPRECIATION FOR GOD'S WORD.

A Lamp Unto My Feet, a sequel to *The Walk of Repentance*, is a 12-week journey through the beautiful Psalm 119. This practical, personal study is a great resource for any individual seeking guidance in the midst of life's struggles. Through daily meditation readings and questions for reflection, believers will be asked to consider the truths of Scripture. At each week's end they will also read about the life of David, a man after God's own heart and author of this epic psalm. Every reader will be brought into a deeper love, respect and appreciation for God's Word.

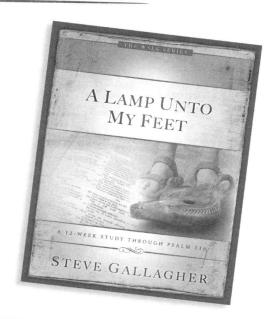

Pressing On Toward the Heavenly Calling

A 12-WEEK STUDY THROUGH THE PRISON EPISTLES

THIS TWELVE-WEEK STUDY OF EPHESIANS, PHILIPPIANS AND COLOSSIANS WILL INSPIRE EVERY BELIEVER TO KEEP "PRESSING ON."

The Prison Epistles are a divine archive of profound revelations about the kingdom of God, accumulated by a man who for many years enjoyed unbroken fellowship with the Lord. For nearly thirty years, the "apostle to the Gentiles" had been pouring out his life and pointing multitudes to Christ. Now, his life and his letters come alive in a practical and personal way. Through this twelve-week study, every believer will be inspired to join Paul's quest in *Pressing On Toward the Heavenly Calling*.